SLEEPWALK WITH ME

and other painfully true stories

MIKE BIRBIGLIA

Simon & Schuster
New York London Toronto Sydney

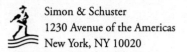 Simon & Schuster
1230 Avenue of the Americas
New York, NY 10020

First Simon & Schuster hardcover edition October 2010

SIMON & SCHUSTER and colophon are registered trademarks
of Simon & Schuster, Inc.

For information about special discounts for bulk purchases,
please contact Simon & Schuster Special Sales at
1-866-506-1949 or business@simonandschuster.com.

The Simon & Schuster Speakers Bureau can bring authors
to your live event. For more information or to book an event,
contact the Simon & Schuster Speakers Bureau at 1-866-248-3049
or visit our website at www.simonspeakers.com.

Designed by Nancy Singer

Manufactured in the United States of America

10   9   8   7   6   5   4   3   2   1

Library of Congress Cataloging-in-Publication Data
Birbiglia, Mike.
  Sleepwalk with me and other painfully true stories / Mike Birbiglia.
    p.   cm.
1. Birbiglia, Mike. 2. Comedians—United States—Biography. I. Title.
PN2287.B45463A3 2010
792.7'6028092—dc22   2010018393

ISBN 978-1-4391-5799-2
ISBN 978-1-4391-7565-1 (ebook)

To my parents, Vincent and Mary Jean.

If it weren't for your support of my many delusions, I

would not have been able to write this book.

Also, don't read the chapters about yourselves.

Also, I love you.

CONTENTS

It's January 20, 2005, and I've just performed at a college in Walla Walla, Washington. Now I'm staying at a hotel called La Quinta Inn. Some people correct me when I say that. They're like, "No, it's La Keeen-tah." I'm like, "That's not fair. You can't force me to speak Spanish. I didn't press 2."

I'm asleep, and I have a dream that there's a guided missile headed toward my room and there are all these military personnel in the room with me. And I jump out of bed and I say, "What's the plan?" And the soldiers say, "The missile coordinates are set specifically on you." And I say, "That seems very bad."

Well, the only difference between this dream and any other is that I literally leapt out of my bed, because a few years before that I had started walking in my sleep.

SLEEPWALK
WITH
ME

DON'T TELL ANYONE

I'm sitting at a Starbucks in Manhattan. Starbucks is the last public space with chairs. It's a shower for homeless people. And it's a place you can write all day. The baristas don't glare at you. They don't even look at you. Every once in a while they walk around with free samples of banana-chocolate something. "No thanks. Just the two-dollar coffee"—cheapest rent in New York. Plus, they sell CDs and even Christmas gifts. If this place sold toilet paper, I probably wouldn't have to shop anywhere else.

Well, the reason I'm writing is that I want to tell you some stories. And they're true. I always have to point this out because whenever I tell stories, people ask me, "Was that true?"

And I say, "Yeah."

And they say, "*Was* it?"

And I don't know how to respond to that. I guess I could say it louder. *"Yeah!"*

"It's probably true. He said it louder."

Growing up, I was discouraged from telling personal stories. My dad often used the phrase "Don't tell anyone." But not about creepy things. I don't want to lead you down the wrong path. It would be about insignificant things. Like I wouldn't make the soccer team and my father would say, "Don't tell anyone." And I would say, "They're gonna know when they show up to the games and I'm not on the team and I'm crying."

One time I built up the courage to ask him about this, which was tough because my dad is a very serious man. He's a doctor—a neurologist. When he's home, he spends most of his time in this one armchair reading these thick war novels. My dad goes through war novels like I go through boxes of Cinnamon Toast Crunch.

So I built up the courage to ask, "How come you play everything so close to the vest?"

My dad said, "The more people know about you, the more they can use it against you."

This sent shivers down my spine because it had that kind of open-ended fear to it—like that feeling you get when you're driving and you see a cop. And you're not speeding. You don't have drugs. But you're just thinking, *I hope he doesn't notice I'm driving.*

Once in a while I told personal stories at the dinner table and my father would say, "Hush!" I'll give you an example. In grade school, I was a terrible reader. We used to do these things at school called Student Reading Assignments, and the teacher would post on the wall a list of how many everyone had done—which is a great way to squash a child's self-esteem. I remember there was this girl in my class named Jamie Burson who finished 146 of these things before I finished 2. And I distinctly remember thinking, *I might be retarded.* And then I looked at the wall and thought, *Oh yeah, I am.*

So one night, I sat at the dinner table and said to my dad,

"I think I might be retarded." And he said, "Hush!" Which is one way to address a problem—just keep it under wraps.

That's what my father would say whenever anyone told uncomfortable stories. So I developed this habit of telling uncomfortable stories.

So here goes . . .

I HAVE SOMETHING TO SAY!

The earliest memory I have of getting widespread attention was at age five when I was shitting in my backyard. I don't want to set a dirty tone for this book, but it's precisely what I was doing. Shitting, that is. The logic at the time made perfect sense. Our dog Duffer shat in the yard. Duffer and I were friends. We were also treated with roughly the same amount of respect. I had the urge. So I just pulled down my pants on the periphery of the woods (which is where Duffer did it too!) and laid one down. About four seconds into it I hear "Michael!"

That was my mother.

Then I heard laughter. That was my brother Joe and our neighbor Leslie. The thing about shitting in the backyard is that word travels fast. That's a quick, easy story to tell: "Mike Birbiglia shat in his own backyard. Yes, like a dog."

JD Howarth lived across the street to our left. Mean, dangerous, and my brother Joe's age (four and a half years older than me), JD had nicknames for everyone in the neighborhood. He called my sister Patti "Pat Pat Patterson." He called my brother Joe "Jew-sef" (we're Catholic). He called Gina "First Class Weiner-Burger" (not that similar to her name or persona, but catchy). He called our neighbor Amy Wall "Small Wall" (clever). He had a special name for me.

In addition to shitting in the backyard, I had peed on Mrs. Jarvis's lawn on several occasions. Mrs. Jarvis lived across the street from us and she didn't want us anywhere near her house. As a matter of fact when we rode our bikes and big wheels on the sidewalk in front of her house, she came out and shouted at us, "Get off my lawn!" She must have had motion sensors on and around her lawn, because the moment you entered that space, Mrs. Jarvis was there.

When my mother came out and explained that we weren't on her lawn, Mrs. Jarvis explained that she owned the sidewalk. *She owned the sidewalk?* That was a strange claim: owning a public sidewalk.

Well, I'm not sure what happened next, but I ended up peeing on Mrs. Jarvis's lawn. I think I knew the response peeing would garner and was using it as a weapon. Well, Mrs. Jarvis was not happy about this. I mean, she thought she owned the sidewalk. My attack did not go unpunished, however. Mrs. Jarvis got a spotted lawn, but I got a nickname from JD: "Tinkles."

The summer after eighth grade, my friends Pat, Nick, and Eric invited me to Old Mill Pond to jump out of a tree into water. This is something they had been doing for a long time on their own. They had never invited me because they didn't see me as a jump-out-of-a-tree guy. They did not think this was in my wheelhouse of skills. And they were right. My skills, at that point, included making English muffin pizzas, microwaving hot chocolate, and dipping English muffin pizzas in hot chocolate.

So I'm standing in a tree thirty feet above the pond with my three friends and my friend Pat says, "Dude, jump!" And I look down at the water, which is so far away, and I say, "That doesn't seem like a good plan." And they said, "Dude, we already jumped, it's no biggie. What's the worst thing that could happen? It's only watah" (that's "water" with a Boston accent), which is really flawed logic, that watah logic. I learn later that many bad things historically have happened in water. Shark attacks. Drowning. Bad sex. But my friend Nick makes an argument that in Massachusetts is irrefutable. He's like, "Do it." So I do.

And at first it's going pretty well. And I start thinking, *Hey, maybe I am a jump-out-of-a-tree guy!*

And then two things happen. The first is that my back lands flat on the water and it makes a gunshot noise. The second is that about nine gallons of water rush so far up my ass that it feels like it's coming out of my mouth. It's like a back alley colonoscopy from Dr. Old Mill, whose instruments had been sterilized in frog piss and pond scum.

Underwater, I can hear laughter coming from above the surface and I think, *I can hear that. It must be loud.* I get out of the water and roll around on the ground, trying not to cry while explaining to my friends how much pain I have just experienced. But they won't stop laughing. This is the funniest thing they have ever seen.

I enjoyed the laughs, but I knew there had to be an easier way to get them.

· · ·

So I knew I wanted attention, but I didn't have any skills. At our family dinner table, it was difficult to get in a word edgewise. Every once in a while I'd shout, "I have something to say!" And everyone would look over. But I didn't have anything to say.

I didn't fare any better at school. I wasn't the "class clown." The class clown was always the mean guy who walked into class and said, "You're fat! You're gay! I'm outta here!" Our class clown was Eric Smart. He'd pull his dick out in gym class and whack people with it like it was a wet towel. And those kids would cheer. They'd be like, "Yeah! He hit me! Eric's hilarious!" And I'd be like, "He's not hilarious. He's elastic. That's not a skill. That's an attribute."

Since I wasn't as freewheeling with my anatomy, I needed to develop my own act.

In eighth grade I took Mr. Bobbin's science class. Mr. Bobbin was in his second year of teaching, and the word on the street was that his first year hadn't gone so well. According to one story, one day when Mr. Bobbin was writing on the board, everyone in the class threw pennies at his head in a vicious premeditated attack. One of Mr. Bobbin's problems was that he wasn't great at expressing anger. So he turned around and said, calmly, in his strangely high-pitched voice, "Could you please stop throwing pennies at my head?" He should have been like, *What the fuck is wrong with you? You're throwing pennies at my head? Are you serious?*" Then he should have flipped over a few desks, ripped open his shirt, pounded his chest, and shouted, "Don't fuck with Mr. Bobbin!" That would've shaken everybody up. Like, "Mr. Bobbin's crazy. I think he might murder us!" His milquetoast response, however, made the kids want to torture him even more.

Mr. Bobbin's class was divided by tables. My tablemates included Alison Dibuono, who was adorable, and Andy Mc-Greevey, who was this musclehead who wore the same pair of Toughskins every day and mentally didn't seem all there. Sometimes he would look off into the distance and chuckle like a character out of *Apocalypse Now*. And with his personal hygiene, no one liked the smell of Andy McGreevey in the morning, or in the afternoon. Andy was known for his ability to start little fires in the woods, and had parents who would give him large outdoor knives on his birthday. He put them to use, carving his initials into high school property, and turning sharp sticks into even sharper spears.

I had a crush on Alison but really had no chance. The juniors and seniors had swept up Alison immediately upon her entry into Shrewsbury High School. High school is not unlike a Mormon fundamentalist cult where the women are claimed by the older and more powerful. Alison would say things to me like "You know who Joe Barrett is? He's on the varsity baseball team. Isn't he cute?" And I'd have to swallow my pride and say, "Yeah, he's cute!" This was the best I could do. I concealed my heterosexual impulses and played the role of gay best friend.

I could make Alison laugh, however. And that was exciting. After we got the word that Mr. Bobbin couldn't handle his students, we did whatever we wanted to. We wouldn't listen. We would carry on full conversations during lectures. I had this completely pointless bit where I would crawl on the floor when Mr. Bobbin was looking away and hide in different parts of the room. Eventually Mr. Bobbin would say, "Has anyone seen

Michael?" And Alison would play along. She'd say, "I think he's in the bathroom, Mr. Bobbin." And then when he wasn't looking, I'd pop back into my seat, and he'd turn around and say, "Michael, where were you?" and I'd say, "I think I was in the bathroom." This killed with Alison. And made me want to push the envelope further.

Taunting Andy McGreevey made Alison laugh a lot. Although because he was something of a live wire, I never knew what his response would be if I made fun of him. He might laugh a little. He might flip out and then shout something at me really loud, which would get him in trouble with Mr. Bobbin, which was again funny because Mr. Bobbin's nonthreatening high-pitched admonitions were hilarious. Around this time, I started watching *Saturday Night Live* religiously and doing terrible impressions of Dana Carvey's impressions of George Bush. Another popular character at the time was Jon Lovitz's "Annoying Man." Annoying Man would come on Weekend Update and make excessively irritating nasal sounds and stick his fingers near Dennis Miller's face until finally Miller would say, "Annoying Man—please!" and then Annoying Man would exit. It was hilarious. And my impression of it was terrible. Regardless, I used to do that impression in Mr. Bobbin's class. I didn't have a Dennis Miller, so I used Andy McGreevey, not as well known for his straight man work but frankly, I didn't have a lot of options.

So one day in the middle of a lecture, I'm sticking my fingers in Andy's face and ears and making these awful nasal sounds and Alison is laughing, hard. So I just keep doing it. "I'm Annoying Man and I like to touch your ears and they're all filled with wax and your hair has all this grease . . . " And then Andy punches me in the face—hard!

My nose starts bleeding.

And it fits in perfectly with the anarchy that is Mr. Bobbin's science class. Mr. Bobbin turns around and with utter passivity squeaks, "Michael? Why is your nose bleeding? You'd better go to the nurse." At this point, my face is a bloody mess; Mr. Bobbin is confused; Andy is pretty happy with himself. And the whole class is laughing.

All was well in the world.

My quest for attention ran into a serious snag when, at thirteen, I decided to go to St. John's—an all-boys Catholic school.

The first few weeks overwhelmed me because there were all these kids from different towns: Shrewsbury, Worcester, Sutton, Oxford, Milford, and Leominster. (Or as we say in Boston, "Shrooz-bray, Wuh-stah, Suh-ehn, Ocks-fuhd, Mil-fuhd, and Le-min-stuh"). It was my first taste of the real world, and the real world didn't like me.

Overall, I'm not sure that my sense of humor translated at St. John's. I had a few small victories early on. I took a French class taught by a great teacher, Monsieur Girard, and his only rule was that you *had* to speak French. So as long as you spoke French, you could get away with just about anything. One day he asked me to read a passage aloud where one of the characters shouts at another character, *"Dansez!"* (Which means "Dance!") And the other character has *no choice* but to start dancing. This struck me as very funny, so in the middle of reading this, I had the impulse to look up at Monsieur Girard and say to him, *"Dansez! Dansez!"* to which he had no choice but to start dancing. And then I got up and started dancing. It was an artistic atrocity but a funny breather in the middle of a boring day.

I started to shout *"Dansez!"* regularly in the middle of class, and Monsieur Girard, a good sport about this, indulged me for a while. At a certain point, however, it became not funny anymore. But that didn't stop me. I carried on. And I noticed that sometimes it would be funny again. I began to experiment with David Letterman's rhythm of saying something so many times that it's funny, then not funny, then funnier because of the shared experience of its not being funny. Ultimately, I did okay in French. My comedy, that is.

I quickly discovered, however, that in the athletic community, absurdist comedy didn't really fly. Generally the "You're fat! You're gay!" oeuvre of humor prevailed. And instead of fighting it, after a while I gave in and tried my hand at it.

My fellow soccer players and I constantly called each other gay. A common conversation would be like "Yo-uh gay." "No, *you* ah." "No, *you* ah."

That would last an hour, and would provide at least five minutes of laughs. Every day, as we walked down the hill to soccer practice, we'd have a back-and-forth between the soccer and football teams that the other team was gay. So what developed was this all-out "yo-uh gay" war. I later found that one of my "yo-uh gay" grenades landed on a guy named Joey Grigio. Now, I didn't know Joey Grigio. I still don't. But he was from Worcester. He was tough. Liked to fight. He was like a cross between a white Allen Iverson and a velociraptor.

So one day I'm walking down the hill to soccer practice and I'm hit by what feels like a rock on the back of my head.

I later found out it was a fist. (I forgot to mention: Joey Grigio had rocklike fists.) And the impact of the hit knocks me to the ground immediately. So I'm on the ground, being hit by the rock-fists again and again, until finally I'm like, *I need to run away*. I don't even consider fighting back. I'm just like, *I have to leave here . . . This is going terribly . . . This is the worst walk ever.*

So he hits me four or five times. Mind you, he's in full football gear and I am in nylon shorts and shin guards. If he had wanted to beat the crap out of my shins, no dice, but really anywhere else on my body was fair game. So I run down the hill. And he shouts, "Now who's gay?"

At this point it occurs to me that Joey Grigio actually cared that someone called him gay. It never occurred to me that calling someone gay had any meaning. We called everything gay: the football team, some of our teachers, the water fountains, geometry (in fairness, geometry *is* one of the gayer maths).

So I try to go on with business as usual, but that day, in the middle of sprints at practice, I start crying. And when the coach asks me what happened, I tell him. So he talks to the football coach. And at this point, I assume Joey Grigio will be punished in some way—maybe expelled, suspended. But he isn't. He's suspended for one football game. I was shocked. They caught the guy who attempted to smash my brains in, and they were like, "Oh, don't worry about old Joey, we're putting him away for a long time—forty-eight minutes to be exact, plus halftime."

So Joey gets one less game of football, which I thought was nothing. Apparently Joey didn't feel that way. So he sent some of his fellow velociraptors after me.

One day I'm at my locker and this guy Bill Murphy says,

"Hey Mike," and I look over and he punches me in the face. Not *really* hard but enough that it makes the punch-in-the-face noise and he says, "That's for Joey Grigio." I was the victim of a walk-by punching, the younger brother of the drive-by shooting. I was stunned. I thought, *Wait a minute. This guy's smaller than me.* And I didn't even fight back. I just thought, *I guess this is what my life is going to be like now.*

The next day I'm in the computer lab writing an article for the school paper about the aviation club and this guy walks in and he says, "Dave Garson's looking for you and he's not happy." And I'm like, "I don't even know who Dave Garson is." This is my situation. I'm the kind of person, who, for fun, writes articles called "Aviation Club Soars into Orbit!" and an unhappy bully I've never heard of is sending out *envoys*.

A detail that made this entirely strange was that during all this violence everyone was wearing a coat and tie. That was the dress code. So these bullies were pretty dressed up. They looked like low-rent child mobsters sent in to threaten people on faulty loans.

Well, I made it through the winter and I decided that I was going to stick it out. Like all great underdogs, I had been knocked down but I was going to make a place for myself. So I ran for class president. And I lost—badly. I came in ninth out of ten. Not ready to throw in the towel, I tried out for the tennis team. And I didn't make it. St. John's just didn't want to participate in my life. And so at the end of the year, I come up with a different plan. Which was to quit.

I ran this by all the adults in my life: parents, teachers, my guidance counselor. And what's surprising is that not one of them used those clichés they say in afterschool specials: "Don't do it,"

"Stick it out," "Don't let 'em get the best of you." They knew the best of me was off the table. Everyone knew it. Somehow I had become the fall guy for the entire ninth-grade class. I symbolized a certain kind of kid, the kind of kid *everyone hates*. So I left.

At my new school, we had those first few weeks where everyone's getting to know each other: "Where you from?" "What was your last school like?" And I decided to omit the fact that at my previous school I had been picked on so badly that I left the school. And you know what? They never found out. Here's a truth about life that they never tell you in those afterschool specials: running away works—for a while.

Fifteen years later, I'm on stage at the Mohegan Sun Casino. I'm a professional comedian and I'm performing for an audience of professional drunks. It's actually going pretty well, all things considered. But there is a four-top in the front row that won't stop talking. It's two tough-looking guys and their dates. And they're talking as though there's no kind of show going on at all. Full volume. Almost distracted by my pesky monologue when trying to make key conversation points. So I politely say, "Hey guys, if you want to talk, maybe go in the other room." This is my typical strategy for people who don't understand the etiquette of watching a standup comedy show. I sort of mention it offhandedly as though it's a misunderstanding.

Well, they didn't pick up on this social cue and they continued talking. And I tried to continue but every few jokes I'd go to hit a punch line and one of the guys' voices would peak and the audience would hear some combination of my voice and this guy's voice, a sort of unintended douche bag duet. So finally I got frustrated and I implied that they might want to leave the show altogether with their dates, who I implied were hookers. By implied, I mean I told them to leave the show with their hookers.

At this point, one of the gentlemen looked me in the eye and said, "I'm going to fucking kill you."

And I'm looking into this guy's dark, stern eyes and realizing by the seriousness of his tone and the slickness of his outfit that he is possibly in the mob or into some kind of organized crime activity. It takes a certain type of person to threaten your life in a custom-tailored suit. Fortunately, at this point, the doorman intervenes and asks these folks to leave. Crisis averted. I don't have to respond to this gentleman's statement regarding my death.

Later that night, I'm with my brother Joe having drinks at the casino bar.

He's scolding me for what I said onstage. "You can't just call people's wives and girlfriends hookers," he said.

I said, "I know, Joe. But sometimes I'm up there and I can't control what comes out of my mouth."

Right then a couple of women come up to us and say, "You guys lookin' for dates?" We look up and realize that they were the mobster dates from the show.

They *were* hookers.

And it's not outside the realm of possibility that the men in those nice tailored suits *had* thought about killing me and had the means to do it. In retrospect, I probably shouldn't have called those guys' dates hookers, but I had something to say.

DELUSIONAL

When I was a kid, I wanted to be a rapper, a comedian, a poet, a professional basketball player, a country singer, a break-dancer, or the owner of a pizza restaurant where third graders could hang out.

Break dancing was the least realistic of these early goals. I mean, first of all I'm not good at it. I have no flexibility and very little rhythm. On the other hand, I did have some large pieces of cardboard in the attic above my parents' garage as well as a mix tape called *Awesome Summer '82*. But even if I'd gotten my popping and locking figured out, it's really hard to pay rent with a day's worth of nickels thrown at you on a subway platform. But I didn't know all that on the blisteringly hot summer day in 1984 when my siblings took me to see the movie *Breakin'*. I was only six, but since I was the youngest of four kids, my mom had finally given up on asking questions like "Is this movie appropriate for a six-year-old?" Instead she just asked my sister Gina, "It's a full two hours, right?" We climbed out of the station wagon and our mom sped away.

Inside the theater I was instantly sold. I was just like those urban teenagers who break-dance competitively. And besides, my older siblings and I were *the only* people in the theater aside from a mother and her son. So we danced along with the movie. First we break-danced in the aisles, and when no one objected to that, on the carpet separating the screen from the seats. We break-danced our asses off. Everyone had a great time, but I had an epiphany: *I'm a break-dancer! This is what I do. My dad's a doctor and I'm a break-dancer.*

My siblings were completely behind me. The next day they invited their friends over to our house and said, "Mike, show them your break-dancing moves. They're so good." And I was off to the races. I started flopping around on the floor, my legs were flying around in the air. And everyone was laughing and having a great time. I was so good I didn't even need music! It was my first brush with live performance. And delusion.

I was a big dreamer and never particularly good at anything— a real dilemma. I wasn't terrible. I was just . . . okay. If you're terrible, you can write everybody off, like, "I don't know what the hell those idiots are doing?" I knew what those idiots were doing. And I knew that they did it better than me.

In the third grade I was selected to compete in the fifty-yard dash at the town track meet on behalf of St. Mary's School. The town track meet brought together kids from our town's three enormous public grade schools—Spring Street School, Patton School, and Beal School—and St. Mary's, my tiny Catholic grade school. My best friend Matthew Sullivan had won all the qualifying events held beforehand at school, but it was school policy that he could only choose one for the town track meet. That way, more kids could participate. It's kind of like the same policy they have at the Olympics. Regardless of this technicality, it was a huge honor to be named to the St. Mary's squad.

For a third grader, the Shrewsbury town track meet is the most cosmopolitan event in your life. There's an ice cream truck. The black family is there. There are tons of those public school kids that we Catholic school kids had been warned about. From an early age we had been told that public school kids were rapists and people who would stab you for looking at them the wrong way. Public school kids heard from their peers that we were fairies. Unfortunately, the word *fairy* rhymes with *St. Mary*. And *rapist* doesn't rhyme with anything.

At the time I had it in my mind that I would defeat these stabbers and rapists in the fifty-yard dash, because I was the fastest fairy of them all. No one bothered to tell me that my tiny Catholic grade school was invited to the town track meet only as some sort of token gesture. It was the public school administrators' way of saying, "We don't hate you Catholic people. Come, let's watch our children run faster than your children." No one told me that my school usually finished dead last. And I wasn't even the fastest fifty-yard dasher in my class. In retrospect, maybe they were impressed with my tiny legs and tendency to uncontrollably flail my arms. Perhaps Sister Mary Elizabeth thought, *Hey, he gets those arms flailing fast enough, something good could happen.*

My parents believed in me too. The night before the track meet my mom made a big pasta dinner—because everyone knows that the secret to winning the fifty-yard dash is massive helpings of fettuccini Alfredo, accompanied by unlimited salad and breadsticks. I went to sleep with a dream of victory.

Race Day: on the drive over to the track, my parents stop

at the drugstore, not to pick up some performance-enhancing drugs, but to grab some M&Ms. My parents figure the right combination of pasta and candy will allow me to overcome eleven years of physical mediocrity.

I show up at the track meet and the whole town seems to be there. I see the athletes are assembled on the grass inside the track, and I head toward it. A coordinator directs me to my group, and I spot the four people I'm running against. I see that one of them is Calvin Walker. He's smiling and stretching out his long legs. I can see that he's wearing special running shoes. I look down at my Zips. I'm concerned. Calvin is not nervous. This is a guy who knows how to run, a guy who has run before, on purpose. And I'm thinking, *This is one of those guys who runs for fun, and not just because his older brother is chasing him with a tennis racquet around the backyard or because he thinks he can catch the ice cream man and get a Chipwich.*

It dawns on me that I need to reset my expectations. It doesn't matter how many M&Ms I eat, I am not going to win this race. In fact, not only am I not going to win, but it may appear to the casual observer that I am not even running in the same race as Calvin Walker. People are going to think that I'm some kind of fifty-yard dash equivalent to the ball boy in tennis. At this point, my only hope is that maybe these other losers in the race are slower than me. I even start planning the outcome, like, *Calvin will get first, I'll take second, that guy is third, that guy will take fourth, and that other loser will be fifth.* Little do I know that these other losers are thinking the same thing and their reality is much closer to the truth. Because when the starting gun goes off, all those losers disappear, and I'm left spinning in a puff of smoke like Wile E. Coyote.

About twenty yards into the fifty-yard dash, I'm losing by about ten yards. I've never been great at math, but I'm losing by twenty percent of the total race distance. So twenty yards into the fifty-yard dash, I do what many quitters and fakers have done before me. I run off the track and grab my toe, hopping up and down in faux pain.

And to make matters worse, I stuck to my story for so many weeks afterward that even I started to believe it. *Why had my damn toe given out? Old age? Not enough toe stretching?* Whatever it was, I returned to fairyville like most fairies did: trophyless. In retrospect, I should have told everyone that the kids from public school had stabbed my toe.

Every kid who grew up in the eighties in Massachusetts thought they could be Larry Bird. The legend of the Celtics superstar was that he was not a natural athlete. Apparently, he wasn't even very good at basketball growing up. He was frankly kind of an idiot. As the legend had it, Larry Bird was just some dumb, oafish kid who had put his mind to basketball. I thought, *That's like me! I'm an idiot and I suck at sports too! I'm exactly like Larry Bird! I'm going to be in the Hall of Fame.* These legends of Larry Bird failed to mention that Bird was six foot nine and had hands the size of baseball gloves.

So I set my mind to it.

I asked my parents to put a basketball hoop in the driveway. So they did. It was on the garage. And since the cars needed to get under it, they placed the hoop eleven and a half feet high, a foot and a half above regulation. The legend claimed that Larry was the first guy to practice and the last guy to leave, hitting free throws until he was nearly blind. So that's what I did. I'd hit free throw after eleven-and-a-half-foot free throw until I was blind. Or I should say, until it was dark. I was really good at playing basketball alone: baskurbation. Surely my solo basketball skills would blow the other kids' minds when I showed them off.

Pat Salazar's dad was a cop. He was a terse, solid man who looked like he might have played college basketball himself. And when I was in fifth grade, he invited a herd of Pat's friends to play basketball at Dean Park. It was the first time I'd be able to strut my stuff. Let the mind blowing begin.

Warming up, I knock down a few jump shots. I throw up some free throws. Looking good. Then we pick teams and the game begins. Right away, a new teammate passes me the ball and I attempt a shot, but Nick Spinelli immediately stuffs me. I turn to Mr. Salazar, "Foul?"

"No way. Nothing but ball."

That must be a fluke. That guy's a great defender. Nick may just be the Magic to my Larry.

Moments later the ball comes to me again on the perimeter and I throw up another jumper. Stuffed. Turnover. I'm beginning to lose the support of my team. *I'm sure Larry dealt with this all the time.* After two more of these getting stuffed moments, Mr. Salazar pulls me aside and explains that the problem is my stance. "Look, Mike—you're about five feet tall and these other guys are about five six, and you're shooting the ball from just below your chest." He shows me how to stand and launch the ball from just above my head. "Like Bird," he says. Now he's speaking my language. I'll shoot my jumpers like

Bird. Soon I'll be in the NBA and then the Hall of Fame, and on the side I'll be a professional break-dancer. All thanks to you, Mr. Salazar!

When the game resumes, I'm passed the ball and I attempt another shot, this time with this new "Larry Bird" style. And this time I'm not stuffed. But a very unusual thing happens. My shot does not reach the height of the hoop nor travel the distance between me and the hoop. It looks like I'm playing a different sport altogether, like volleyball. Or shot put. Or some kind of British sport I'm not familiar with. That's when everyone starts laughing and I start crying. I find that you really lose the confidence of your fellow basketball players when you cry in the middle of a game. They will not throw you the rock when they see tears streaming down your face.

The next time I call for the ball, shouting, "I'm open!" they give me this look like, *We know. We're well aware of your openness.*

"There's nobody covering me!"

We wouldn't either if we were on the other team, which we wish we were.

At the next water break, Pat Salazar asks if I'm hurt. I play it off like I am. "Yeah. Yeah. I think it's my elbow." But the truth is I'm not hurt. No one fouled me. No one even came close to fouling me. *I wish they did. I could have shown off my free throw.*

My professional basketball plans may have been cut short by the reality of opposing players, but as long as *sharks* still rhymed with *parks,* no one could convince me that I couldn't be a professional poet or rapper. And when the Shrewsbury police department visited St. Mary's School to conduct their "DARE to Keep Kids Off Drugs" program, I saw the opportunity to launch my career as a rap star who also happened to hate drugs.

Looking back on it, could there possibly have been a more confusing acronym for trying to keep kids from experimenting with drugs than *DARE*?

"Kids, we're here today to DARE you not to do drugs! We DARE you to accept our DARE!"

"Officer, does that mean you want us *not* to do drugs, or to *do* drugs?"

"We DARE you *not* to do drugs!"

"But I thought we weren't supposed to do things we're dared to do. If you dared me to jump out of a tree, I shouldn't do that, right?"

"It's just an acronym, son."

"What is an acronym?"

It was confusing, but I still got a free DARE T-shirt, and the day before we were to receive our DARE certificates of completion, I took the chance that could ignite my fledgling rap career. I approached Sister Mary Elizabeth and proposed that my friend Eric and I perform a two-man rap song called "Bust Them Drugs," a takeoff on Young MC's popular hit "Bust a Move." Originally there wasn't going to be a talent show portion of the event, but I thought a parody rap song with all-new lyrics was in order, and for whatever reason, she thought that was a good idea also. Maybe she had the foresight to realize that twenty-two years later I would need a ridiculous anecdote for my book to demonstrate what an attention-starved delusional maniac I was, or perhaps she thought it would buy her another five minutes to sit in the back row with her eyes closed reconsidering her lifelong commitment to Christ.

If Young MC had happened to walk into the basement of St. Mary's School on that spring morning and witnessed Eric Marciano and me prancing around with microphones, screaming our made-up lyrics to "Bust Them Drugs" over his 1989 hit "Bust a Move," he would not have been impressed. We were a good three or four bars behind the beat, repeatedly referred to our notes for lyric reminders, and since we didn't have the instrumental version, our lyrics collided with his actual lyrics, quite harshly. Even Eric and I, who thought we were pretty good, realized that our rap performance would have to be cleaned up a bit before we headed out on tour. We'd also need to get an instrumental version of "Bust a Move."

To be a comedian you have to be delusional. I think it's because the human brain can't process the amount of judgment that an audience casts upon you when you do standup comedy. If you're in a play and it doesn't go well, the audience thinks, *We didn't like the script, or the set, or the costumes.* In standup comedy, there are two hundred strangers in a room thinking, *We don't like* you. *All this stuff that you're about—we're not into it.* To become a comedian you have to tell yourself it's going quite well, otherwise you wouldn't get on stage the next night. You'd just think, *I guess human beings don't like me.*

I can't even describe my first time doing standup. I was in a contest and it felt like I was under anesthesia. I came off stage and asked my friend, "How did it go?" And he said, "You're gonna be okay." I do remember the second time.

One of the judges of that contest was a comedy club booker/restaurateur named Evan. He asked me if I had a car. I didn't, but my girlfriend Abbie did, so I said, "Yeah."

He said, "I can set you up at a place called Fat Tuesday that will pay you $50 if you can perform thirty minutes of comedy."

What I should have said was, "I only have about eleven minutes of material." What I did say was, "Perfect."

I drive Abbie's mint-green Ford Taurus to Fat Tuesday, one of those days-of-the-week restaurant chains: T.G.I. Friday's, Ruby Tuesday, Ash Wednesday's, Holy Thursday's. Fat Tuesday wasn't as much a comedy club as it was a bar that had a comedy night. Frankly, "comedy club" is a pretty subjective term to begin with. To have a comedy club all you need is a bar and a wall of eight-by-ten photographs of comedians. Actually, they don't even have to be comedians, just people in black and white looking zany.

I'm nineteen years old and I show up at Fat Tuesday. I look up at the wall of photos of people who may or may not be comedians and think, *These people must be geniuses. How do I get my picture on a wall like this?* I try to pick out the famous ones—the Chris Rocks, the Jerry Seinfelds, the George Carlins. They are not on this wall. It's like being handed a stack of old baseball cards and flipping through them trying to find the Reggie Jacksons or Pete Roses, but it's just all Felipe Orlandos and Dan Pasquales. Optimistically, I think, *These must be the real comedians. The underground guys who are the real deal.*

So now, thoroughly intimidated by the headshots of Katherine Clousterbom and Ted Finklestein and his red puppet

Fiddlesticks, I'm whisked backstage—backstage being the side-walk of a strip mall. I'm scared to death because they've agreed to give me fifty dollars for thirty minutes of comedy. And I know that I do not have that.

I ask Matt Marcus, the comedian I'm opening for, "Hey, what happens if I run out of material?"

"Just make fun of people."

I say, "I don't know if that's going to go so well. Whenever I do that, people punch me in the face."

"You're the one with the microphone."

I don't understand. Am I supposed to hit people with the microphone if they try to punch me?

I've discovered since then that making fun of audience members is an entire genre of comedy. Comedians have entire acts that consist of pointed nuggets like, "Nice shirt, faggot!" To which the people around that gay-shirted audience member reply, "It's so true! His shirt *does* suck! This guy's a genius!"

I'm standing on the sidewalk, holding a 3×5 index card with five bullet points. I'm desperately trying to figure out how I'm going to stretch this into thirty minutes. It says: "Stick Insects. Cookie Monster. A-Team. Teletubbies. Millionaire. Slash."

This was the material:

Stick insects

I'd hate to be a stick insect because all the other insects are always bumping into you because they don't know you're there, and you have to be like, "Watch it." And they're like, "Yeah, you look like a stick." And you're like, "I have eyes." And they're like, "Yeah. They were closed."

So that's stick insects. That'll last three to five minutes.

Cookie Monster

I'm not sure if Cookie Monster is a great role model for kids. I mean, do you think this guy might have an eating disorder? He only eats cookies, and the back of his throat is sewn up. The cookies just kind of fall off his face. Who is that guy kidding?

That's the whole joke, there. That's gotta take up about five minutes.

A-Team

I love that show *The A-Team,* but sometimes I get the sense that they weren't really trying. If you're on the run from the law, you might want to go easy on the gold chains and feathers. Maybe take the red stripe off the van . . . Just a couple of ideas.

We're probably somewhere past twenty minutes now.

Teletubbies

I just read that Jerry Falwell was upset because he thinks the Teletubby Tinky-Winky is gay. And I'm like, "Which one *isn't* gay? Is it Dipsy or Laa-Laa?" Like, "I think Dipsy and Laa-Laa are definitely heterosexual, living in the Midwest, starting a family, etc., but I have a feeling about that Tinky-Winky."

Nearing twenty-five minutes, I think. Is there time to squeeze in a few last bits?

Slash

I was watching the show *Politically Incorrect* and the musician Slash was on and he was complaining that there was too much violence on television. His name . . . is Slash.

I'm staring at my notecard and it's dawning on me, this is definitely not thirty minutes. And then the manager opens the door and says, "Mike, go." I turn around and throw up on the sidewalk. It's like my body can't take it and is like, *What do we do? Let's get rid of some food!*

I walk through the door. And the guy on the loudspeaker says, "Please welcome Mike . . . Ba . . . hooski!" which is really not even close to my name. I'm so mad. I think, *You didn't even try. You just said* B *and then whatever you could think of and you made me Polish and that's a really specific choice.* I stand on stage and perform four minutes of comedy to complete silence. It's almost as if these people haven't watched *Sesame Street, Teletubbies,* or *The A-Team* in years.

I walk off stage and apologize to the audience under my breath. The manager calls me into his office. And I'm so nervous. It's just me and this strange man in his office the size of a telephone booth and I fear the worst: *Does he have a gun? Is he going to punch me?*

He doesn't.

He takes out fifty dollars and hands it to me. And I say, "Thanks," as though that gun scenario has never crossed my mind.

He says, "Can I ask you a question?"

"Sure."

"Do you have an eight-by-ten photograph of yourself?"

"No."

"Can you send me one?"

"Okay."

I drive home and I know what I have to do if I want a comedy career: I need to get an eight-by-ten photograph of myself immediately.

At one a.m., I walk into Abbie's apartment and she asks me, "How did it go?"

I pause, and think for a moment. And then I say, *"It was amazing."*

PLEASE STOP THE RIDE

In seventh grade, people started making out with each other. This was very upsetting to me. I didn't even understand the concept of making out. I was like, *People we know are making out with other people we know? But how?*

My sex education to that point had been minimal. I had certainly always been interested in girls, but I wasn't so sure they were as interested in me.

Leslie Saliba lived across the street from our house when I was four. Two years older than me, smart and pretty, Leslie was "the girl next door," both in the way she'd be characterized in Hollywood and in her location. She was the first of a string of women in my life who have viewed me as a very good friend.

When Leslie and I became friends, I was so young that I could barely speak. I'd call her on the phone (which was absurd because she lived seventy yards from my house), and if she wasn't home, I'd let the phone ring endlessly, while staring across the street at her driveway waiting for one of her parents' cars to pull in. I was three; I did not have a lot of other appointments.

"Hello?" (Out of breath.)

"Can Leslie come out and play?"

"What? No. Leslie's not home, Michael. Leslie will call you later." I wouldn't wait until later. I'd call back in about forty minutes. It felt like four hours.

When Leslie and I did play, usually we'd walk in the woods and Leslie would invent fantasy scenarios. Queen-servant. Princess-ogre. Occasionally we were fellow explorers, but even then I would take the fall. She'd make a mud pie (out of dirt, not chocolate) and ask me to taste it. I would. I was the same person who shat in the backyard.

Leslie and I played almost every day for the better part of seven years, after which Leslie went to middle school. I'll always remember the day she came home and said to me, "I met a boy."

And I thought, *I'm* a boy. But I said, "Cool." I knew I didn't stand a chance with those middle-school kids. I was Tinkles.

Around the corner from us lived Jesse Nolan, who was responsible for my sex education from ages nine through thirteen. Jesse was also two years older than me and very wise in the ways of women. At least that's what he told me. He'd say, "I don't know what it is, girls just like something about me. I can't put my finger on it." And I couldn't put my finger on it either. Jesse was this hyperactive, eye-shifting, husky guy who used to trade baseball cards with me in a way that left me with fewer and less valuable baseball cards after every session.

One day Jesse took me into the woods behind his house and showed me a stack of porn he had stolen from older kids. He kept these issues of *Penthouse* and *Hustler* in tree trunks, not the most weather resistant of hiding spaces. So we'd leaf through pages of soggy old porn. This was my first experience with nudity other than my own. The closest I had come to seeing a woman naked was in the *Sports Illustrated* Swimsuit Issue. Since my parents never gave me a sex talk, all I knew was that sex had something to do with swimming.

Jesse had a discrete furnished basement and a TV with HBO, which in the eighties played soft-core porn around 2:30 a.m. So if we could coax our bodies to stay up with the help of candy and soda, we would find ourselves watching a film that might or might not have a woman in skimpy or no clothing. Sometimes we got burned. One time we stayed up late to watch *Candy Stripe Nurses*. The description in *TV Guide* was "Young sexy nurses and their hospital adventures." *Perfect. Adventures! We know what that means, right?* Well, their adventures weren't all that sexy. Take for example "Marisa," who was ordered to do volunteer work as a punishment for assaulting her teacher. She fell for a young man accused of knocking over a gas station and did some investigating to try and clear his name. And then there was Dianne, who fell for a basketball player, whom she tried to talk into giving up drugs. Those were not sexy adventures but quite thoughtful. I felt like the filmmakers had played a trick specifically on sexually frustrated insomniac twelve-year-old boys.

One summer Jesse introduced me to masturbation. I was in his furnished basement when he put on some bootleg porn, got under a blanket and started moving around furiously.

"What are you doing?"

"Jerking off."

"What?"

"Grab a sock from that drawer."

"Why?"

"To jerk off."

"What do you mean?"

"Don't you touch your dick?"

"Sure."

"Till white stuff comes out?"

"I think so?" I hadn't. But I played along.

I grabbed a sock, put it on, and then jerked off until white stuff came out. *That was very satisfying,* I thought. *I'm going to do that a lot.*

And I did.

At one point Jesse introduced props into the solo-sex trade. He took out a banana-shaped "vibrating muscle massager" from the Sharper Image catalogue that his dad used for his sore back.

Jesse said, "You can use this."

"For what?"

"To put against your dick."

"Yeah?"

"Yeah. Go in the bathroom and use it. It's great."

"Um, okay."

I went into the bathroom and tried to use this muscle massager. It didn't feel too great. I felt like I had when Jesse tricked me into trading my George Brett rookie card for assorted Boston Red Sox "future stars." Also, in retrospect, I'm pretty sure that massager was intended for women.

So in the seventh grade when people started making out, this came as a complete shock. It just seemed so intangible—like this alien ritual, where these two aliens just attached orifices all of a sudden. I was like, "I am not doing that!" And collectively all the girls in my class were like, "That is fine. You are not on the list. You're not exactly a first-round draft pick for this new activity." Making out always seemed kind of gross to me. It still does. I've always heard this homophobic argument, "I don't like it when I see two dudes makin' out in the street!" I feel that way about anyone. Making out is sloppy. It's like a dog eating spaghetti.

The only prerequisite for a makeout party was a furnished basement, a two-liter bottle of Fanta, and a Debbie Gibson CD. I remember kids I had known my whole life suddenly started making out with each other. It was as though this had been their plan all along. Like there was this secret conspiracy. "Once we're twelve years old, we're going to just start making out with each other. But don't tell Mike Birbiglia. He might try to get involved." Everyone I knew was losing their mouth virginity.

These makeout parties took place about once a month and one by one I lost my closest friends to the makeout club. For a while, my closest ally was Matthew Sullivan. We would regularly write off the members of the makeout club: "Making out is stupid." "Frenching is for losers." (Since when do kids know anything about French culture?) I felt like one of those kids who proudly wears a chastity ring but secretly hopes that someone will just start having sex with them. So Matthew was in the non-makeout club with me. Informal, of course. There were no meetings of the non-makeout club. Those would be sad meetings. "I call this non-makeout meeting to order. First order of business: Nintendo. Second order of business: *Why doesn't anyone like us?*"

So Sullivan and I were in the non-makeout club, but I knew it was only a matter of time. Michelle Calandria was on his tail. Michelle planned an end-of-the-year birthday party, timed with a New Kids on the Block concert she had gone to the night before. Romance was in the air, and Matt would need every bit of strength he had to hang tough.

I remember being in Michelle's basement, listening to "Stairway to Heaven" and pouring myself a cup of Fanta with no ice. I looked up and saw Matthew Sullivan locking lips with Michelle. Next to them was my friend Eric Marciano making out with Margaret Billingsley. I had lost two friends in one night. I still don't like Led Zeppelin to this day. I try to intellectualize it, but I think the truth is I'm still angry that they created an eight-minute makeout anthem that separated me from friends I had known my entire life.

The non-makeout club was lonely. I started thinking, *I want to be part of the makeout club.* My only prospect was Lisa Bazetti, an adorable girl I'd become friends with—thanks to an alphabetically ordered seating chart. We spoke daily on the phone about homework and one time I made her laugh. And I thought, *I gotta do that more.* So I did. And then at one point I got her laughing so hard, she said, "You gotta stop, I'm gonna pee myself!" It was the closest I had ever come to a vagina. I spent the next fifteen years trying to get Lisa Bazetti to pee.

Lisa had many suitors; Tim, Rajeev, Jeff, and me. I was in fourth place in all the trade publications—*7th Grader Weekly,*

Middle School Monthly, Pre-Teen Beat. Lisa was a popular gal, always on the verge of peeing. One night when we were on the phone, I built up the nerve to ask her to go to the carnival. And she said yes.

So this was going to be it. My night. I would play a carnival game and win her a stuffed bear larger than her bedroom. Then we would make out. Simple.

When you're twelve years old, you don't understand certain things about the digestive system. For example, you don't know that you shouldn't eat popcorn and peanuts and cotton candy and then go on a machine called "the Scrambler." Cotton candy is of course the most absurd of those items, almost as if the inventors said, "We're going to take sugar, which everyone knows is bad, but then we'll *dress it up* like insulation."

And the general idea of the Scrambler is that you sit in a two-person pod with the person you are in love with—and that pod goes in a circle—which is part of an even grander circle—which is part of an even grander circle.

As I understand it, it was originally designed as a medical device for constipated patients, and it was called the Shitzyourpantserator. And then the Carnival Workers of America, CWOA, co-opted the Shitzyourpantserator. And they said, "We feel like the name is something of a turnoff."

And then somebody suggested, "What about the I-think-I'm-gonna-die-erator?" And they responded, "That's good because it gets at the essence of how you feel when you're on the machine. Plus it has the added word play with diarrhea, which is a nice homage to the original intention of the machine."

And then someone said, "What if we call it the Scrambler?"

And the boss jumped up and said, "Nailed it! But who will be in charge of this dangerous piece of equipment?"

And this one guy said, "Well, I have a nephew who's sixteen years old and smokes pot twenty-four hours a day. I feel like he might be available."

And the boss said, "He sounds amazing. We don't even need to interview him. He sounds completely qualified."

So Lisa and I go on the Scrambler. And from the moment I sit down in the Scrambler and they latch on the bar seat belt, I know I'm going to throw up for sure. The bar seat belt is not a reassuring piece of safety equipment. That is not a Ralph Nader–approved device. I don't think the bar seat belt has ever saved anyone's life, though it has probably pinned someone's esophagus to the pavement in a Scrambler accident, ensuring that the Scrambler victim won't ever talk about the Scrambler accident.

So they latch the bar seat belt shut and I think, *This is bad.* And I even say to the sixteen-year-old stoner, "Hey, actually—" And then he is gone. Apparently he doesn't enjoy the second halves of sentences. So I grab the bar.

And Lisa and I start scrambling. And I know that I'm going to throw up.

And I think, *I need to stop this from happening.*

So I come up with a strategy: Don't look at Lisa and don't look at any other people.

Don't look at Lisa or any other people . . . Don't look at Lisa. Don't look at any other people . . . This plan will not suffice. I need a new plan.

And my new plan is: tell the Scrambler operator that he needs to stop the ride.

But the mechanics of the Scrambler are such that the window of opportunity in which one can communicate with the Scrambler operator is a very short window.

So I think, *I gotta tell the guy to stop the ride. I gotta tell the guy to stop the ride. I gotta tell the guy to stop the ride*—

"Please stop the ride!"

Scrambling . . . and scrambling—*I don't know if he heard me. Maybe I should say it louder. I'm not sure he's even paying attention*—

"Please stop the ride!"

And I'm back to scrambling . . . and scrambling—*He's definitely not paying attention to the ride. I think he might be smoking pot right now . . .*

"Please stop the—"

And then I threw up, not unlike a lawn sprinkler. Just popcorn and peanuts and insulation. Really insulating the pavement with my homemade carnival salsa.

And I didn't look at Lisa. But I'm pretty sure she was staring at me because I was really a spectacle at that point. And I think I dropped from fourth to fifth place on her potential boyfriend depth chart that day. Needless to say, we didn't make out.

The next year I was enrolled at the all-boys school and every year they'd have what people called "a cattle call dance." It basically means the school would invite girls from *all over* the state. It seems like an offensive way to describe something, to imply that women are cattle. *So the cattle's showing up at eight and then we make out with the cattle and then the cattle leave at ten.* Then we'll go get burgers—but that's not part of the cattle analogy.

So the dances were held in this gymnasium charged up with hormones and Binaca and Drakkar Noir. All crammed into a room with strobe lights and Bel Biv DeVoe and sweat. The strobe light is helpful because people can only see you every five frames or so. Strobe lights are really good for hiding acne, braces, leg braces, sweater vests, sweaty armpits, over-the-pants handjobs.

There was no alcohol, so there wasn't any kind of social lubricant. Just warm Sprite and Dixie cups of pretzels.

I went with my friend Sam Ricciardi. He was a makeout ninja. Every week he'd tell me about all the girls he had made out with over the weekend. Usually those makeouts took place at the mall—which seemed perfect to me. I imagined this strange food court orgy. And I'd be like, "Sam, how did that even happen?" and he never really told me. He'd be like, "It's the mall, dude. It's crazy." I was like, *I gotta go to the mall.* The mall sounded like a perfect place because I hadn't had my first kiss, but at an all-boys school you could never admit that you hadn't had your first kiss. So when people asked if I had had my first kiss, I'd be like, "Me? Yeah! Totally." So I was living this lie, terrified that one of these days someone was going to call me out. They'd be like, "Well, what's it like?" And I'd be like, "It's like eating an ice cream cone?" and they'd be like, "No it's not. It's like licking a rocket pop." *Oh man. Wrong frozen dessert analogy.*

So I'm at the dance with Sam and there were two girls our friend Tom had introduced us to. They were the last two cows

at the dance. We were like, *Moooooo!* They were like, *Moooooo!*
It was love at first moo. And it was one of those situations
where guys (and girls) say uncomfortable phrases like, "You
get that one." That follows us all the way from childhood into
adulthood. "That one's yours and that one's mine." Like we're
cars. And I don't feel like I've ever been one of the good cars. No
one's ever seen me and said, "I get that one!" They're more like,
"I get that one? Um, okay." Or even, "I get that one? You owe
me." It's so sad to think that people are incurring debt based on
my appearance. I'd hate to hurt someone's credit score.

So I'm dancing with this girl Sondra and we haven't really
spoken but I think we both have a sense that making out is
about to take place. Maybe it was that magical moment she noticed me staring at her mouth, trying to figure out how I could
land my mouth on hers in a smooth, non-teeth-bumping way.
And we're fast-dancing, which is really hurting my case. I can
tell that she's thinking, *If he's this bad at dancing* . . . So her
interest is waning but I'm saved by a slow song. "Stairway to
Heaven." I knew I had approximately eight minutes to climb
those stairs.

And slow dancing isn't all that challenging. It's just like
hugging someone in slow motion. And all I'm trying to do is
just not fidget, because then it might seem like I'm trying to
start the making out before the making out starts. Because all
it takes is the slightest tilt of the head. Just the subtlest tweak of
the neck and it is on. I think that's one of the things that scared
me so much about the making-out concept. I had kissed rela-
tives on the mouth but never with tongue or the tilt.

And the combination of the tilt and the space in between
the two mouths is what scared me. No one has video footage

of what happens in the middle of those two mouths. It is uncharted territory. It's the giant squid of making out. There's no way to learn how to kiss. There's no kissing camp. There's just camp.

It was that unknown that terrified me. Literally terrified me. What if there was some secret move that no one was telling me about that happens in there, like you swap tongues for like one second or your tongue presses a secret button on the other person's tongue? And then afterward someone is like, "Did you press the button?" And I'm like, "No! There's a button? I really botched this one. I didn't press the button."

So I think, *I have to do this,* so I initiate the tilt and then she comes in strong. It was really like an all-out mouth war. And Sondra had artillery. She had braces. It was like a dog eating spaghetti *and the fork,* because of the braces.

And as this oral atrocity is taking place, all I could think was, *I'm not alone! I'm not one of those freaks who hasn't had his first kiss. When I finish up here I can make fun of those losers!*

And then afterward, Sam asks me, "How'd it go?" and I say, "It went pretty well, actually." And then as days went on I started thinking it went much better than it had. Like, *That was great! I'm great at this!* This could work! So I called Sondra.

But we had nothing to talk about because we didn't know each other, like "Remember when we made out? That was cool, right? Hey—is there a button? Nevermind. I love the show *Full House.* You like that show? Yeah. I hate it too." And a few days later she stopped calling me back. And I was like, *What is up? First I rock her world and now this? I took her for a ride on the Mike Birbiglia mouth machine and now she's not calling me?*

So I say to Tom, the guy at school who set us up, I'm like, "What's up with Sondra?" And he has this shit-eating grin.

And I'm like, "What?" And he's like, "Sondra said you're the worst kisser she's ever kissed."

And I was crushed. The worst part was that I couldn't explain that it was my first kiss because I already lied about it not being my first kiss.

So I had to play it off like it was my style. I said, "Yeah, that sounds about right. I'm a terrible kisser."

Fortunately Sam was right there with me. He smiled and nodded, saying, "Me too, dude. Me too."

Growing up, I was a big fan of the *Indiana Jones* movies. I watched them again recently and found them to be misleading. Aspiring archeologists across the world probably show up to their first day of work with their weather-worn fedoras and their whips and they're like, "Where's the cavern of jewels?" And their boss is like, "Actually, today we're gonna start off by dusting thousands of miles of nothing." The thing I admire most about these movies is the conviction and sense of self that Indy has. He's an archeologist and an overly trusting action hero and he's okay with that. Indy's always like, "My long-lost friend with a glass eye and a black suit needs a hand locating a crystal scepter that turns people into sand? Sure, I'll help. That sounds totally on the level." The other notable thing about Indy was that he always got the girl. I'm not sure this is true for real archaeologists. And it definitely wasn't true for me.

When I was in high school, my parents moved from Shrewsbury, Massachusetts, to Cape Cod, so I was separated from my childhood friends. There was a geographical mid-point between my friends and me at Great Woods, an outdoor concert venue. Basically these outdoor venues are a great opportunity for musicians to play for huge crowds and for teenagers to convert Porta-Potties into meth labs. I attended these types of festivals with much enthusiasm, in an earnest search for who I was.

One summer, when I was seventeen, I decided to wear a cowboy hat, not unlike that of Indiana Jones, to many of these summer concerts, not to seek out treasure nor to put to rest ancient curses, but to prop up a hibachi in a tailgate parking lot and eat salmonella-laced chicken kabobs while getting drunk enough to befriend strangers. What I discovered by wearing this cowboy hat was that people would remember who I was. I was "the cowboy hat guy." And I was proud of that. I was like, *That's who I am! I'm the cowboy hat guy! And no one can take that away from me, unless of course they take the cowboy hat, in which case, they'd be the cowboy hat guy.*

Well, at the time I didn't think it through, so I was the cowboy hat guy.

And one summer while wearing the silly hat at a Steve Miller Band concert, I met this girl and fell in love. Well, I thought I fell in love. I actually just found her physically attractive and so attributed to her every positive quality I'd ever hope for in a woman. We ended up making out on the lawn of the Great Woods Center for the Performing Arts. For me, it was great. For the people watching, it was awkward, pathetic, or *totally totally hot.* But I went home with her phone number and address and I proceeded to write love letters to her. Or, I should say, elaborate fictional narratives that ended with the two of us reuniting in some strange way that included one of my heroes like Jimmy Connors or Bill Cosby and somehow we'd get to the next Steve Miller Band concert just in time for the encore of "Fly Like an Eagle."

Well, after a summer of letters, I built up the courage to call her.

She was having a slumber party with all of her friends and so I spoke to the whole group. And it didn't go as well as I had hoped. There's something about women in groups. And beyond that, there's something about women in groups on the phone that generally leaves the male on the other end of the phone at a severe disadvantage.

They decided to read excerpts of my letters aloud and after each excerpt there would be an eruption of laughter like a Johnny Carson highlight reel. None of my letters included jokes, but they seemed to bring these girls great joy. At first I was happy to be the hit of their party. After just a few of them I said, "Okay, well, I'm going to go now, that's funny . . . I guess if you read it like *that* it does sound a little silly . . . I think I have to go to the store now with my brother . . . okay, good-bye!" A few weeks later, I started my senior year and I hung up my cowboy hat. I didn't know who I was. But I knew who I wasn't.

I had my first girlfriend, Amanda, during my senior year of high school. And she was great. She was beautiful and she played tennis. And she wrote for the newspaper. She was a bad girl, and I was kind of a dorky nerd, but not even a mainstream nerd, because this was at a boarding school that I didn't board at. I was only there because my family lived nearby.

This was a big deal for me because it was the first time I fell in love and thought, *Oh, there is someone for me. This is it. I found her.*

Amanda had major street cred.

She had been expelled from her previous school for dealing acid. At one point she told me, "It was totally messed up because it was actually this other girl who was dealing acid and I was framed." And I was like, *Awesome.*

I thought it was one of those things where we were opposites and we knew it. And that made it *more* exciting. Like she wanted to be a writer and in student government and I wanted to know what it was like to be cool.

I find that when you fall in love, you overlook certain red flags.

One of them was that she was a liar.

I don't mean that in a pejorative way. At boarding school lying can be a way of life. There was one legendary liar in my class named Keith Robbins. He used to lick his finger like a bookie and say, "Yeah, yeah, nice. Nice. Nice." He would lie about things that weren't important. One day he said, "Yeah, yeah, nice, nice. My uncle is Tony Robbins, the motivational speaker. Yeah." And I found out later that it wasn't true. But even if it were, it wasn't that impressive so you didn't bother protesting it. You'd just go, "Oh, okay, Keith."

Another red flag was that Amanda would say really mean stuff to me, and then try to pull it back. She'd say, "You're not good at *anything*—only kiddin'!" "Nobody likes you *at all*. Just jokin'!"

The final red flag was that she told me not to tell anyone she was my girlfriend.

She explained to me that she had another boyfriend at home that she was in the process of breaking up with. She assured me it was over, but if it got back to him, "You know, it'd be bad." I totally got that.

So she would go home every weekend and visit him, and at one point she said she had to go home more frequently because his parents were sick, so she had to console him. And I thought, *Well, you know, the guy's parents are dying. So I ought to be understanding.*

I also put up with it because I couldn't believe how lucky I was just to be with her. When you're in a relationship with someone who's selfish, what keeps you in it is the fact that when they shine on you, it's this souped-up shine. And you feel like you're in the club. And you don't even know what club it is. You just know you want to stay in it.

We'd been going out two months and we went on Christmas break and she invited me to meet her parents in New Hampshire.

This was very exciting. This was going to be my big moment. It would legitimize me as the main boyfriend.

So I drive my mom's Volvo station wagon from Massachusetts to New Hampshire. And Amanda introduces me to her parents as her "friend Mike," and I can see how she's playing it. She doesn't need to put a label on me. I totally get it.

And then this guy shows up.

And his name is Scott.

And the three of us are hanging out. It slowly dawns on me that I'm hanging out with my girlfriend's boyfriend.

And it's going *okay*. He seems like a good guy. He's an all-state wrestler and remarkably nice. I could totally see what she saw in him.

It hurts but there's some consolation because every time he steps out of the room, she's very affectionate toward me. She kisses my neck or says something in her sweet voice.

But then there's a moment when I was in the bathroom, and I think, *What's happening in the other room?*

The day takes an even stranger turn when Scott suggests that we go hang out at his house.

And so we go and I meet his parents. And it's a very strange thing meeting your girlfriend's boyfriend's parents for the first time. Part of you is angry for obvious reasons and part of you still wants to make a good impression. On a side note, they seemed in perfect health.

I drive home, defeated. And I sort of know at this point that this is her life, and I'm her secret life, like on Maury Povich.

So I think, *This is it. I'm going to stick up for myself. It's either him or me.*

And I convince myself that given that choice, she would choose me because what we have is so special. So when we get back to school, I call her and say, "We need to talk. Let's meet at the hockey game."

And she says, "Great!"

So I go to the hockey game. And she's not there. Hockey game ends. Still no sign.

I have this pit in my stomach because I'm going to tell her that she has to pick me or that's it. But I can't find her. So I start walking around the school, to the library, the cafeteria, the places she might be. And I ask people where she is. And finally someone says, "I saw her with Keith Robbins down at the tennis courts."

I remember earlier that day, at lunch, Keith said to me, after licking his fingertips, "I'm sleeping with your girlfriend. You know that, right? Yeah. Yeah. Nice. Nice."

And I thought, *Well, I haven't even slept with my girlfriend, so that would be insane. And second of all, he's a liar, so he must be lying.* I remember I said to him, "Yeah, I know."

But at this moment it dawns on me that Keith is her new second boyfriend. And I'm done. And it's that horrible lonely feeling where you're walking around someplace and there are people all around and there's only one person you want to be with, no matter how mean that person has been to you. I just want to hear that "Only kiddin'!"

People are coming up to me and I can't even hear them. I can't even tell them what happened because even though I'm being dumped, the relationship itself is based on a secret.

And that spring I graduated.

Keith Robbins was expelled for making fake IDs in his dorm room. He had built an enormous driver's license from Arkansas that people stuck their face in. And he would photograph them, and then laminate it. He later took a job at Goldman Sachs. That detail seems made up, but it's actually true. Nice.

Amanda was expelled the next year for dealing Ritalin. I'm pretty sure she wasn't framed.

At boarding school, you can't go to the graduation if you're expelled. It's one of the shames of being expelled. And it's very strict.

I found out later that Amanda actually did show up to the graduation. In a disguise. She wore a wig and sunglasses.

My friends laughed about this story when I told them finally, the way friends do to make you feel better when you've had your heart broken. But I could relate to her doing that. Because sometimes when you want to be in a place so badly, you'll do anything.

GODDAMMIT

Being a dad has never appealed to me. It doesn't seem like a job you'd apply for:

> Screaming child seeks adult man to pay for his entire life.
> **Warning:** When the child is fourteen he will tell you he hates you and forget about everything you've ever done for him.
> **Requirements:** Must have sex with your wife or girlfriend without birth control at least once. Also, your wife or girlfriend will hate you through most of the pregnancy, for a few years afterward, and intermittently for the next twenty years. **Pay:** No pay. **Education:** Grade school or equivalent. **Benefits:** Your child may bear some likeness to you. Also, if you take your child on walks, other women will be more attracted to you than you've ever experienced in your life, but you can't have sex with them unless you want your wife (and children) to hate you even more than they already hate you, which is intermittently or always.

Dads always seemed mysterious to me. Matthew Sullivan's dad had an eighteen-foot motorboat in the backyard that never worked in the fifteen years I visited their house. We used to play hide and seek in it. *Why was he keeping this boat that never worked?*

Pat Salazar's dad was a state cop; every time he spoke, it felt like you were being arrested. I'd be over for dinner and he'd say, "Patrick, how was the pancake breakfast at St. Mary's?" Pat would answer with trepidation in his voice—as though there were a right or wrong answer, and he was hoping to feel out the right answer as he went along, watching his dad's every facial expression for clues as to which way he wanted his son's answer to go.

"It went . . . great?"

"Good." His dad nodded, as if to say, "You're free to go."

I never saw Pat's dad release the kind of fury that everyone anticipated, but it sure as hell seemed like *someone* had seen it.

If I were to shoot a movie called *Dads,* it would feel a lot like *Jaws,* where you rarely see the shark, but there's always a sense that the shark is coming and when he does, you best get yourself to the shore.

My dad was no exception. But I was more afraid of my friends' dads than of my own. Because when your dad starts going off, you know what he's capable of. When your friend's dad starts going off, you're like, *This guy's a wild card. He just kicked the dog. What do you think he's gonna do to us?* There was this kid named Alex in my friend Eric's neighborhood. And Alex had done something wrong one day when we were playing across the street. We didn't even know what it was. And when Alex's dad came home, he started yelling at Alex, and Alex's response must not have been adequate because Alex's dad started punching him. Right on the doorstep. He held on to his sweatshirt while he slapped his face and punched his chest. The ol' face-chest punch-slap.

We didn't get involved with that punch-slap minefield. We were safely on Eric's front steps. That was our property, kind of. I cautiously said to Eric, "Do you think we should do anything?" And Eric, holding back tears, said, "That's just what Alex's dad does. I don't want to talk about it." Understandable.

My dad never said a lot when I was a kid. And when he did, I'd get worried, because it probably meant he was mad about something. It's hard for people who have jobs where they are in charge to come home to anarchy and chaos and a family where no one listens to you. At work, he could say things like "Scalpel," and someone would hand him a scalpel. At home, he'd say, "Someone find me a rake," and I'd shout, "I'm not finding a rake. I'm watching the Celtics!" That wouldn't go over so well. In instances like these, my dad would shout so loud it was like a rock concert. It was like a Dad-tallica concert. It shook you to *your core*. Even if the rock-and-roll shouting hadn't made a sound, the sheer magnitude of the vibration would get you up to get that rake. *"WHEN I SAY GET A RAKE, YOU GET ME A GODDAMN RAKE! THESE GODDAMN KIDS NEED SOME REALITY TESTING!"*

My dad has always been obsessed with "reality testing." I didn't know what the hell he was talking about, but apparently we needed it. I guess it meant we were living in some kind of fantasy world. It didn't seem like I was in a fantasy world. At school Matt Backman would call me a faggot six times a day and regularly throw me down a cement hill. *What the hell kind of fantasy was that?* If my life was a fantasy, it would have things like girls liking me back and a dad who didn't shout so loud it made me wince.

Once, we were preparing for a Christmas ski vacation to

Vermont. And my dad never bothered to make sure the rusty old ski rack fit our newer car. So when that freezing morning came, he realized that we needed a new rack and it would cost three hundred dollars or more. "We're not going, goddammit!" He was literally canceling Christmas. I was petrified. Now we'd have all that excess pent-up anger in our own house for all of Christmas instead of letting it run wild in the mountains.

But my brother Joe, always resourceful, realized he could strap the skis to the roof of the station wagon with bungee cords, just like in the olden days, and the vacation was back on.

Joe wasn't as intimidated by our dad. Somehow he was oblivious to it all. I think because he thought of Dad as another guy, not this larger-than-life stoic whose every word was chock full of meaning. Joe's casual attitude toward our parents grew as he did. During his first visit home from college, he started addressing my parents by their first names: MJ and Vince. It was as though he had taken some course about the oppression of names, and he decided to take charge, to throw off the shackles of "Mom" and "Dad," like these titles represented some form of indentured servitude or something. Or maybe he just did it because he thought it was funny. It was a little bumpy at first. MJ, whose full name is Mary Jean, was fine with it. I believe her response was "That's my name!" Vince was not so keen on being addressed like he was some sort of golfing buddy.

I couldn't believe what Joe was doing. I was fifteen years old and I asked Joe, "You can just call them MJ and Vince?"

And Joe said, "I can do anything I want." He was right.

Every time Joe would say, "Hey Vince!" my dad would frown at him, give him a long judgmental stare, and then, if

Joe hadn't yet backed down in this staring contest, Vince would throw in the word *"Enough."*

That worked in the short term, but Joe was persistent. The nicknames eventually stuck. Now we all call them MJ and Vince. It's pleasant. "Mom" and "Dad" always felt a little stodgy.

Vince isn't stodgy, but he's certainly a bit formal and definitely private. He's a doctor, and on top of that, he picked up a law degree in his spare time, for kicks. Vince is the kind of guy who knows *stuff*, which is intimidating because I'm the kind of guy who knows *nothing*. Well, not nothing. But we know different types of things. Like my dad knows the hemispheres of the brain and I know that if I spill Diet Coke on my laptop, it probably won't start again. Which is why I think my dad was so disappointed when I became a comedian. He worked his whole life to send me to college so I could learn stuff. And I didn't. And then I got a job making fun of him in front of strangers. His whole plan kind of backfired.

Vince spends most of his free time at a fancy golf club. This runs in stark contrast to his upbringing. He grew up in Bushwick, Brooklyn, the son of Joseph Birbiglia, the original Joe Birbiglia. Joseph Birbiglia Senior ran a luncheonette in Brooklyn and during the Depression was a union electrician with crews digging subway lines. I recently learned that he often had to use a fake name to hide his Italian heritage.

When I was a kid my dad occasionally said cryptic things like "There's a lot of prejudice against Italians." Which was confusing for me because I hadn't experienced any of this prejudice at St.

Mary's School or at AJ Tomaiolo's Restaurant. They hadn't made me stand in a separate line or disguise my name with some kind of ethnicity-free shortening, like "Birdman" or "Birthdayboy." Because my dad always said so little, he sometimes left out the whole story: "There was prejudice against Italians *in the thirties*."

My sister Patti, who has spent some time in Sicily, where the Birbiglias are from, traces my dad's temperament to Sicily. She claims that the streets of Sicily are filled with Vinces, suspicious of everyone but members of their immediate family. And for them, Vinces reserve a special kind of suspicion.

Growing up, whenever my dad got annoyed or felt taken advantage of or slighted for any reason whatsoever, he would yell, "Fine, I guess I'll just *send the check*!" and storm out of the room.

But when he played that card a few years ago, my grown siblings and I were all like, "We kind of get our own checks now. Are you still sending out checks? I feel like you might have the wrong address for me. Can I get direct deposit?"

My whole life, the thing that struck me about my dad was that he was always in control. He drove the car. He decided where we'd spend Christmas. And he knew, or pretended to know, how to do anything that needed to be done. This all changed when personal computers became popular.

Since high school I've had sort of moderate computer skills. My parents never got involved with personal computers until everyone they knew had a personal computer. That's how they knew it was safe. They literally might have been the last people to join the digital age. In 1997 I sat next to my dad and showed him how to use the mouse on my iMac. He tried it for about two minutes, and then turned to me, scoffed a little, and said, "Well, these are never going to catch on."

I think it was the concept of email that really sold my dad on the need to have a home computer. For as long as I can remember, my dad would call the house several times a day and ask, "Any calls, any mail?" Now that there was a new kind of mail that someone somewhere might be sending him, he had to know about it. So they finally rolled the dice and purchased one of these newfangled contraptions that would never catch on.

Shortly after college, I stayed with my parents for the summer and became their full-time, on-location tech support. I had previously done a lot of this work on the telephone:

ME: Okay, do you see a file on your desktop that says, "Ten ninety-nine underscore Int"?

MOM: I don't see that anywhere. What is a desktop?

ME: Like, when you turn the computer on, the stuff you see on the screen, that's the desktop.

MOM: It says here, "I cannot find the disk drive!"

ME: What? Where does it say that?

MOM: In huge black letters.

ME: On the desktop? On the computer screen?

MOM: It's written right here on this Post-it note. Your father wrote it, and he stuck it to the desk, so I guess it's on the desktop, yes.

Again, I know very little about computers. I know how to create Word documents and surf the net. I had no idea how much I knew about computers until I met my parents.

Learning about email has been the big step for my folks. My mom's got a few of those friends who forward everything. And it's okay when you get the email with the fifty cutest puppy pictures of all time, but when your mom forwards you emails like "Pepper is poison and other things the government doesn't want you to know," you gotta step in and be like, "Mom, you gotta tell your friend Martha that pepper is not poison."

For a while, my parents thought every email was written directly to them. They were a spammer's dream. One day my mom said, "My friend Elizabeth at USAirways.com says I'll get five hundred bonus miles if I send FTD flowers through USAirways.com."

"Mom, who's Elizabeth at US Airways?"

"Elizabeth, she sends me emails with special deals from US Airways. I think she's the vice president of marketing."

"And how do you know her?"

"We email each other."

The computer virus was a really difficult concept for my dad to take in. I think because he's a doctor and he knows about real viruses. I remember him asking me, "But where do these viruses come from?"

And I answered as best I could. I said, "I don't know, some crazy hackers in Malaysia write these programs that travel around the world, infecting millions of computers."

And he had this facial expression I'll never forget, like he was confused and sad and furious all at the same time. And he said, "But why?"

It was kind of like a fourth grader asking why there are wars.

"Trust us, kid. It makes sense."

One of the few things I know about computers is that you

should never open attachments that you receive from strangers. My parents did not receive that information. They just click on every email attachment they get. They're like, "We've got mail! Who is it from? XRXRzebars@monkeys.tv! A new friend!"

MJ and Vince ended up with a porn virus that was so nasty it took over their entire computer. The wallpaper, the screensaver. The icons became dildos. A strange man jumped onto the screen and shouted, *"Where's your daughter?"*

My parents were very saddened by this, because when they picked up their computer at Circuit City, they had not thought this was one of the possibilities.

So my Mom called me into the living room and she couldn't bring herself to tell me about the virus specifically. She was like, "Michael, something happened with the computer."

And I've seen some porn in my time. Some accidentally, some not so accidentally, but this was some really hard-core, truck-stop-style porn. And I've had some bad gigs before, but it must be really degrading if you work in porn and the only work you can get is being featured in a computer virus. And you go to the mall, and some guy sees you, and he asks, "Where have I seen you before?"

And you have to ask him, "Has your computer ever been infected with the 'me_love_u_long_time_nude_sex' virus? Because I'm on the twenty-third pop-up window having a threesome with two bald clowns. You can't miss me."

The porn virus made things very tense in the Birbiglia household that week. It seemed like MJ and Vince were suspicious of one another—that the other person had *ordered* this rapid-fire pop-up porn service for the computer. They were double-checking credit card statements. I wouldn't be surprised if MJ shot an email to her friend Elizabeth at USAirways to ask her if this had happened to her too.

It was also particularly awkward because I had never even talked to my parents about sex, never mind my porn preferences. The closest my dad ever came to bringing up sex was when I was in college and I had my first serious girlfriend, my dad stared at me cryptically for a long time and said, "You're playin' with fire."

That was the entire conversation.

That was it.

In the end, I figured out how to get rid of their porn virus. I Googled "porn" and fortunately there were a lot of results, like 60 million. Then I Googled "porn virus" and there were some answers and, finally, an antidote. But my parents still insisted on putting the computer in the corner with the screen facing the wall like the computer had done something wrong. And we've never spoken of it since.

My dad is a neurologist, or a "head doctor" as I always explained to people. When I was a kid, I didn't know what that even meant. I thought it meant if you got a scratch on your head, he patched you up. I had no understanding of the implications of a brain injury or degenerative brain diseases or anything. I just thought it was cool he sometimes saw college football players and even some guys who went to the NFL. Once he was quoted in *Sports Illustrated* in an article about Holy Cross star football player Gill Fenerty.

The article was called "Canada's Hot Southerner," and here's the quote: "A few months later Fenerty underwent more tests. 'We did the arteriograms, CAT scans and myelograms again. They were all normal,' says neurologist Vincent Birbiglia. 'The significance was that there was no underlying structural or vascular abnormality that would be likely to rupture again. I didn't think Gill was at any greater risk of having this occur than any other player.'"

Which begs the question *When did* Sports Illustrated *get so sciencey?* Nowadays if you read an article about a football player, they write, "And his brain got smashed around like a sponge, you know, like the kind you use to wash your truck." And then there's a picture of a truck.

All I knew was that Vince carried his case of medical tools out of the house every morning and returned home around seven for some quiet time. In third grade we had an extracurricular event every Sunday called "science club." That's just what I needed in my life. More science. Every week a different parent would come to one of the classrooms at St. Mary's School and talk about how their job related to science and teach some sort of lesson. We had people who worked in computers and physical therapy.

Toward the end of the series my dad agreed to come in and speak. I didn't know what was going to happen. Was he going to set up a chair in the corner of the classroom, read a war novel, and scowl? Yell about how people had taken certain sections of the newspaper? I was extremely nervous. It was the closest I had come to public speaking myself. I told my friends it would be pretty boring and uneventful. I was managing expectations.

My dad showed up with the mysterious case of tools I had

seen in his car for all those years. He took them out and put them on the teacher's desk in the front of the room. He had the kids gather around and he went one by one through all of them and described what each of them did. He seemed very comfortable. He even pulled out some charts of the body and the brain and had all kinds of explanations that were confusing and impressive. At the end of his speech he took questions and it was clear that he knew exactly what he was doing. It was amazing. I had the smartest dad. I couldn't believe how smart he was. And I couldn't help but wonder why he hadn't told me any of this stuff sooner.

LIKE HELL

One thing about my mom is that she makes up sayings or at least uses phrases that people no longer use. I realized this when I entered the adult world and I would repeat expressions that my mom uses and people were like, "What are you *talking* about?" When I was a kid and I wasn't allowed to do something, my mom would say, "Like fun are you doing that." Which was really confusing because it seemed like she was encouraging me. She'd say, "Like fun are you going to the mall!" I'd be like, "Yeah! Like fun—pizza, buddies, arcade games!" At a certain point, I figured out that "like fun" is a euphemism for "like hell" because my mother is Catholic, and for Catholics, hell is fun.

I love talking to my mom. I'll talk to her on the phone for hours but regardless of how long the call is, at the end of it she'll always say the phrase "one more thing." But it rarely deserves to be "one more thing." It's always like, "One more thing—Ellen from my swim class bought a rice cooker." I'll say, "Mom, that's not a 'one more thing.' In long division that's called a 'remainder.' You save up ten of those, we're gonna give you a conversation!"

For a while it looked like I might become a priest because I was really good at being Catholic and it was this thing that my mom and I had in common. Of anyone in my family, I relate most to my mom. Like me, she's a talker. She'll say anything to anyone in any context. I was visiting my parents recently and I met my mother at the bank and she had been talking to the bank teller for fifteen minutes about really personal things, and I walked in at the end and all I could hear her say was, ". . . And here he is now!"

My mom and I are kindred spirits, so when she sent me to Catholic school, I was thrilled to join the team. And I loved being on the team. Being Catholic was fun. When you're seven years old and your parents send you to Catholic school, your world makes a lot of sense. You wear your little plaid bow tie every day, and your blue button-down shirt with the short sleeves. Every girl in your class wears the exact same patterned plaid skirt. And you assume that everyone in the world is named Fitzgerald, Murphy, or Sullivan.

At Catholic school a lot of your teachers are nuns, and they're always talking about this guy Jesus who everybody's afraid of but everybody loves, because he loves everybody. And a long time ago some people killed him, and it's not *totally* your fault, and don't be scared or sad, because he's living forever, next to God, who's his dad, even though he is also God. And also there's this Holy Spirit part too, that no one really understands. But all three of these guys are everywhere, at all times, just in case you need to talk anything out.

"Am I going too fast for you, seven-year-old boy?"

"Oh, you have questions?"

"Oh, we don't know the answer to that, that's part of the mystery."

"No, he's different than Santa. That's just some horseshit we made up. This is the real deal."

And it's funny how they roll it out to you when you're seven. They're like, "There's this guy Jesus, and he totally loves you."

And you say, "Oh, okay, great."

And they say, "And you love him too, right?"

And you ask, "I'm sorry, do I know that guy?"

And they say, "You know, from the picture of the cross? That guy loves you . . . and you love him."

It starts innocently enough, as innocently as man-boy love can start. You just accept that you're in love with a long-haired dude who loves you and spends most of his time nailed to a cross, as far as you can tell from the statues around school. You're seven. What are you going to do?

Then it starts to get a little heavier. When you're eight they just casually throw it out there: "You know, he died for your sins."

And you think, *Oh man. I thought I'd gotten away with stealing that Brach's candy at the supermarket. I guess that Jesus guy took the fall.*

Then a couple years later, you're eleven, and you get the word that Father Grady wants you to be one of his new altar boys. He's seen your work at recess on the kickball field, and he thinks you've got what it takes to snuff out candles, hold a chalice, and not trip and fall on your robe. You're excited. No one's told you that being an altar boy is like being a priest's AV guy, that church is just as boring when you're watching the back of the priest's head as it is watching the front of his head. It's like watching a concert from backstage.

But church was also kind of glamorous. The priests have

these multilayered robes. As an altar boy, even *you* have a robe. A real simple, white one. It's like karate, where you start with white belt and then you get some different color belts once you start kicking some devil ass. I was proud of my robe. I was thinking, *Check it out, ladies. You want one of these? Not so fast. It's going to be a few years before the Church comes around to having altar girls.*

Some of the priests were very cool. This one priest, Father Jacques, had a cool beard and kind of looked like Jesus. He used to hang out with the altar boys like we were his friends. He took us seriously. He didn't talk down to us like the other priests. A year into his tenure at St. Mary's, Father Jacques didn't show up at our church anymore.

"Where'd he go?" I asked my teacher.

"He's at another parish now."

"Why didn't he say good-bye? We would have said good-bye to him."

"Father Jacques is needed somewhere else."

"Will he visit us?"

"I don't think he's going to visit, but we have a new priest coming in."

The new priest was Father Fauvell. He was fat and bitter. Whenever we'd ask him questions, he'd scold us. "You don't have to ask about everything." We heard through the grapevine that Father Fauvell loved to stay up late with the other priests, playing cards and drinking. Maybe he was tired from all that drinking? All I wanted was Father Jacques to come back. But he was needed somewhere else.

• • •

Church had its cool moments. Every once in a while they'd have a guitarist play with the choir. And I was like, *All right! Rock and roll!* And then she'd start playing "Simple Gifts" or "Hosanna in the Highest" and I'd be like, *No! Play the good songs! "Time after Time" or "We Built This City"! C'mon!*

Some of the altar boys got plush gigs like weddings or funerals. That meant the people running the event would throw you some cash. Wedding, maybe fifty dollars. Funerals, maybe ten. Or twenty. You could buy sixty-five packs of baseball cards with that kind of scratch, all because someone died or got married. I never got those gigs. You really had to be hot on the circuit to get those kinds of breaks. Matthew Sullivan got a lot of weddings and funerals. But I didn't care. I wasn't in it for the money. I was in it for the . . . Wait, I'm not sure why I was in it. Oh yes, the smell of incense. Love that burning smell. Also, we got to light candles.

The most frustrating part about being an altar boy is that you can't speak or move. You just have to sit there. I wanted the priest's job. I wanted to get up there, kill with a few jokes that aren't funny, and then shake everyone's hand like Jay Leno or Oprah. It always struck me how much laughter priests got for jokes that weren't very strong. A priest would be like, "Matthew, Mark, Luke, and . . . John Boy!" and people would be like, "Father Patterson is *hilarious!*" I thought, *If he's a priest, I should be a priest. I'm way funnier than him. Plus, I'm never going to have sex anyway, so what are the drawbacks?*

I was a good Catholic kid, though. I knocked out all the sacraments. I went to confession when I was eleven, which had to be a real snoozefest for the priest. "Okay. So you stole a Jose Canseco rookie card from your brother, and when your mom told you to go to bed, you stayed up late and watched *Alf*? Anything at least *a little* exciting?" In retrospect, maybe we should have been turning the tables on some of those priests in confession. "So Father, what have *you* have been up to?"

I always felt that communion was kind of awkward. On one occasion I received a communion wafer from an elderly priest with hand tremors, and he missed my mouth and it fell on the ground. I was like, *Oh no.* It was as if we were in a seafood restaurant and a waiter had dropped three baked stuffed lobsters on the floor. But the priest was on top of it. He just picked it up and popped it in his own mouth. Like he knew that Jesus has a five-second rule.

The other thing that struck me as odd was when you drank wine out of that chalice. Because when I was growing up, during the AIDS scare, people stopped sipping wine from the same cup. Which is kind of weird, because if you got AIDS from Jesus, you would totally get into heaven.

I went to St. Mary's School from grades one through six. And I only got hit in first grade by Sister Mary Elizabeth. She was of the old guard. Smacked you with a ruler if you talked in class. I talked in class. I'm a talker. Actually, the experience that stigmatized me the most was these fund-raisers they used the kids for every year. I'm not making this up: every year they'd hand us a cardboard suitcase full of trinkets to sell door-to-door to strangers. If we sold enough they'd give us a pair of aviator sunglasses. Because that's what third graders need: sexy eyewear.

I'd walk up to people's houses, carrying this box that's the size of my body. The Church was like my knickknacks pimp. I'd knock on doors, and when people answered, I'd say in a high-pitched voice, "Hello! I'm from Saint Mary's School! Perhaps you would like to buy a Daffy Duck pencil sharpener or a 'Kiss the Cook!' pot holder!"

And they'd typically say, "We're eating dinner right now."

So I'd say, "I'm so sorry, but this will only take a few minutes!" Then I'd just walk right into their home and open up shop. I'd offer, "Perhaps you would like a desk set organizer or a popcorn-of-the-month club!"

And they'd say, "Please leave our home."

So I'd start putting the stuff back in, but it never fit in the way they'd initially packed the case. So I'd be smooshing these items on top of each other and scissor-holding the whole thing together and apologizing, "I'm so sorry, I'll be out of your way in just a minute!" After all that I didn't even get my sunglasses. I wasted all this time hawking third-rate goods when I could have spent the time figuring out what the hell the Holy Spirit is.

For a while I thought that I *would* become a priest, right after I finished my careers as a rapper and a break-dancer. I was always considered the most religious of my siblings, the kid with promise in the pursuits of Catholicism. We had family friends named the Barkers who started making regular trips to Yugoslavia because they heard there were miracles going on there. They would come over for dinner and tell my parents all about statues of Jesus bleeding real blood and statues of the Virgin Mary crying. First of all, these didn't seem like miracles.

They just seemed showy. If Jesus had a revelation, I thought, he wouldn't choose to show it through some gimmicky tchotchke you can buy for ten dollars. Second of all, I just didn't buy it in a general sense. In my gut I felt like, *This isn't real. None of this is real.*

I kept it to myself but then Mr. Barker got a public access TV show where he talked about Catholicism, and he was doing an episode about the youth. Knowing from my mother what a Catholic soldier I was, he asked me if I wanted to come on the show as a guest and talk about my faith.

I said, "Sure," but I had serious reservations about it. He asked again and left a few messages, and I kept dodging his calls. I just couldn't make the leap. Sure, I could believe that Jesus was watching me masturbate to *Candy Stripe Nurses* and listening to my sins regarding baseball cards through Father Fitzpatrick, but I couldn't buy into this miracle thing. I wanted to so badly because it was this one thing that my mother and I had bonded over. For a short period of time, we both believed in Jesus and God and the Holy Spirit. All that stuff. And it was amazing. And I felt closer to my mom than I ever had. And then it faded away. So why couldn't I just suck it up and believe?

Shortly after I finished college, my mom developed a condition where, as far as the doctors could tell, part of her spine was pushing into her spinal cord. They weren't one hundred percent sure of what was happening, but she was experiencing chronic pain throughout her body. The best idea this team of doctors could come up with was to perform an operation where they shaved off a small, suspicious-looking piece of her spine. Unfortunately the pain still didn't go away. So my mom was faced with both the original pain and the pain of the invasive operation. She was laid up for months.

I came home and stayed with her. My dad worked long hours, and someone had to be there to administer her pain meds and get her meals. So I did that and it was one of the hardest months of my life. Not just because of all the housework, which I'm not so good at. But because my mom was prescribed Ativan. She was supposed to take it three times a day, but pretty soon she wanted to take it five or six times a day because, as she told me, she was "dying." It's hard when your mother tells you she's dying, because my mother has been the most stable and dependable voice throughout my entire life. She's an eternal optimist. The roof could be caving in and she'd say, "At least we have a floor!"

So when she told me she was dying, even though I didn't think she was dying, I tended to believe her. I said, "I'm not sure you're dying, Mom. Why do you think that?"

And she said, "They know what's wrong with me, but they're not telling me. They know I'm dying."

So I called her doctor. "When my mom says she's dying, is there any validity to that?"

"No, Michael. There's no reason to believe she's dying. She's just experiencing a lot of pain and jumping to conclusions. This is very common. Just make sure she doesn't take too much of the Ativan. It's just feeding her delirium."

So I hid the Ativan and made sure she didn't take too much. And this made her furious. When she noticed this, she started looking around the house in every possible hiding space, saying, "Michael, where is the Ativan?"

And I'd say, "Mom, I can't give you the Ativan."

And she'd look me in the eye with a sternness I had only seen when I was very young and say, "Michael, I am your mother. And if I say get me the Ativan, you get me the Ativan."

And I'd say, "Mom, like fun am I getting you the Ativan." I'd try to make her laugh. But it didn't really work.

The situation got worse. Where at first she had told me she was dying, over time she became philosophical and started theorizing about the afterlife. She pulled me aside on a number of occasions and, as though she had just been given some secret news that she wasn't allowed to share, she said, "I'm going to hell."

And I said, "Mom, you're not going to hell."

She looked at me as though I was naïve. "Yes, I am. You don't understand these things. I'm going to hell." And then she'd start crying. And I'd hold on to my mom like she was my kid, like she had held me all those years when I was a kid and I fell down or had my pride trampled on by a bully at school.

And holding back tears, I'd say, "Why would you possibly go to hell? You're the kindest person I've ever met."

And she said, "There are things that you don't know about that I've done. And now there's nothing that can be done because I'm going to hell."

I'd try to make light of it. I'd say, "If you're going to hell, then we're all going to hell because I had you as the front-runner for heaven. You're heaven's number one draft pick."

She wouldn't laugh. There wasn't a lot of laughing in this period. I'd laugh myself so I wouldn't cry. I didn't want to show any weakness or any fear that she was in fact going to hell.

LIKE HELL

My mom eventually got better. Years later, she still feels pain, but not in the way she did in that period of time. It's rarely discussed in my family. But I've never gone back to church. I can't support an organization that convinced my mother that she was headed for eternal torture. Like hell am I going to a church like that.

PATTI AND THE BEAR

My sister Patti always intimidated me. We didn't seem to have anything in common. She was eight years older than me, and by far the most rebellious of my siblings.

In high school she convinced my parents to chaperone a school trip to Austria. While there, some of our distant cousins invited my parents to their horse farm. Patti showed up at the farm after having been on a drinking tour of some of Austria's finest ale houses. She was fourteen. And plastered. During lunch, my mother noticed that Patti was acting aloof, so she tried to include her in the conversation.

"Look, Patti," she said. "They have horses!"

Patti, with the fury of a British parliamentarian, shouted, *"I hate horses!"*

My mother, stunned, gave her another chance, "You do, Patti?"

Patti reiterated her position, "I really do, Mom. I hate horses!"

At this point, my parents took Patti back to the hotel and my father placed her in a cold shower with all her clothes on. Then they locked her in her room. Pretty tough stuff for a fourteen-year-old, but what else are you going to do with your drunk daughter who so adamantly dislikes horses?

Patti always resented me because as the youngest of four, I benefited from laissez-faire parenting. Compared to the treatment she received from my parents, it seemed as if I had no rules whatsoever. It was as though by the time I had come around, my parents thought, *this whole parenting thing kind of does itself.* On one occasion, my parents told her she couldn't go to an overnight party at her friend's boyfriend's house and she started crying. She pointed at me, and shouted, "When he's fourteen you're gonna let him do anything he wants!" Six years old and completely confused, I sat there like collateral damage. I had no idea what she was talking about, but I could feel the hostility. She was older than me, smarter than me, and seemingly hated me. So I tried to keep my distance.

She did too. Not just from me, but from the entire family. When Patti graduated from high school, she chose the college she'd gotten into that was the farthest away—upstate New York. After college, she moved farther away—Breckenridge, Colorado. This was her final, masterful escape from the oppressive Birbiglia family. She became a ski instructor, a subtle but athletic blow-off to the parents who had put her through college as a classics major. It was during Patti's exile in Colorado that she and I started to connect. One night, while talking with her on the phone, I discovered she had a fascination with bears.

I should point out that *I've* always had a fascination with bears. An obsession really. And Patti is a part of that.

At age eight, I started to have this recurring dream that there was a bear walking in the front door of my house. Literally opening the front door—which is the scariest part: a bear with opposable thumbs. If a bear can open a door, sky's the limit! I don't have a plan for that one. My plan was the door.

In the dream, I hide in the kitchen cupboard with Patti, and it's pitch-black. Scared to death, I open the door a crack to bring in some light and look next to me. Patti is gone and she's been replaced by the bear. And he doesn't kill me but he gives me this coy, Jack Nicholsony look, like, *"Will I kill you?"* And that's when I'd wake up. I had that dream for years.

One of the things that drew Patti to Colorado was her love of nature and animals, though not horses. Coincidentally, she started to have a recurring bear dream where a bear would approach her in the woods. I shared with her my childhood bear dream and we forged a bond.

In college I took my bear interest a step further by watching Discovery Channel documentaries about bears in all of my free time. I could watch these things endlessly. Bears are simultaneously so graceful and so strong. Bears know who they are, but they often don't know who you are, which is why they kill you. I always feel bad for the smaller animals in these documentaries because I know more than they do about the situation. It's like I'm at a bank heist and I'm the guy in the van watching on the monitor and the narrator says, "The arctic fox has only one known predator: the polar bear." And I'm on my headset yelling, "Arctic fox, it's a setup. Get outta there. Tinkles to arctic fox! Tinkles to arctic fox! Put down the salmon and walk out of the building!"

I was talking about my bear fascination with Patti in a phone conversation, and to my surprise, Patti was quick to point out some additional factoids about bears.

"Polar bears can smell their prey thirty miles away."

"Yes, that's true. But black bears are the most ferocious. They're nine feet tall and their claws are as sharp as razor blades."

"Yes, and grizzly bears weigh around 900 pounds and can run up to 40 miles per hour."

These conversations could go for hours.

A few years ago Patti and I decided to meet the bears from our dreams in real life. We went to a place called Katmai National Park in Alaska, a remote park that can only be reached by small four-seat MacGyver-style bush planes that land on the water.

When you arrive you're taken to what's called "Bear Orientation." They teach you that if you encounter a bear, you're supposed to clap and make the bear aware of your presence. You're supposed to shout, while clapping, "I'm right here, bear! I'm Mike and you're a bear and we're cool with each other." When they told me this, I thought, *Oh . . . I'm going to be murdered by a bear because that sounds like basting yourself with barbecue sauce. Like, I'm right here, bear! I'm right here, and I taste fantastic.*

Later that week Patti and I went fly-fishing with a guide. I don't know if you've ever tried fly-fishing, but it's much more difficult than it looks in *A River Runs Through It*. There were salmon jumping out of the water—literally *jumping* out of the water—which is exactly what I would do if I were a fish because that seems like a great field trip. You're in the boring water all day and then all of a sudden you're flying in the air and you're like, *Whoa! I wanna stay here and grow legs and become a human!*—which is what happened . . . over time (sorry, home-schoolers).

So, these salmon are jumping out of the water but I can't get one with the rod because there's this whole technique where you're waving your arms around like an orchestra conductor. If you don't catch one you feel like an idiot because they're jumping in front of you and you're conducting them but not catching them, and thinking, *I should have brought a net.*

I'm not catching anything and the fishing guide feels bad for me. So he catches one himself and then places the rod in my hand and shouts, "Ya got one!" And that hurt my pride, because I knew that I hadn't.

I'm with the guide and Patti is about seventy-five yards behind us and I hear her say, *"Miiike."*

Her voice had a very distinct pitch. It was the voice of a person about to be mauled.

I turn around and see an eight-foot brown bear walking toward her in the water. The whole thing was very surreal because the bear wasn't running toward her like in a horror movie, like *I will murder you!* He was simply walking toward her in that laid-back bear fashion as if to say, *I'm a bear, etc.*

I was proud of myself because I built up the courage to say, "Guide . . . do something!" The guide snapped into action. He ran at the bear and screamed at the top of his lungs, "HEE-AHHH! HEE-AHHH!" And the bear walked away—calmly. He was like, *All right . . . I'm a bear, etc.*

Now, I was very relieved that my sister hadn't been mauled, but I was a little bit mad at the guide. I thought, *You didn't tell me about the "HEE-AHHH!" plan. You just told us to say, "I'm right here, bear!"* It's like he gave me the bad parachute. Like I jumped out of a plane and everyone's chute went off and I had been given the multicolored gym-class-parachute. And I'm flapping this rainbow chute as I fall to my death thinking, *This doesn't do anything! Except build team skills!*

Watching Patti almost get eaten by a bear changed something for me. In that moment, she was no longer the older, intimidating sibling whom I feared as a child. Nor was she the distant rebel who shunned our family. She was bear food. And so was I. It turns out we had a lot in common.

GOING PLACES

My earliest aspiration in life was to sit in the front seat. The youngest of four, I spent most of my days as a kid in the way back of my mom's station wagon as she ferried my siblings to and from school, hit the Worcester Center Galleria Mall, and sometimes stopped by her Gloria Stevens exercise classes. In a station wagon, you've got "the front," "the back," and the "way back." Nowadays the way back is an illegal way to transport children. You're only allowed to transport dogs, groceries, and illegal aliens in the way back, but in the eighties they were like, "The kid'll be fine. The way back is entirely carpeted and safe, except for the spare tire and jack."

The way back was an anarchic wilderness of coloring books, six-month-old Christmas tree needles, and often a lone peach or strawberry, withering away toward a slow death. And since my mom has always driven with one foot on the gas and one foot on the brake, it was a pretty bumpy ride in the way back. But I loved it. The way back was like watching the world as a movie. The rectangular window offered a panoramic view of everything. No one ever knew what was happening in the way back. It was like a separate hotel room attached to the car. I could wave at people. Occasionally moon people. Flip them the bird when I figured out what the bird was. I remember one night on the trip home from seeing *The Nutcracker* in Boston, I made eye contact with a girl about my age who was also sitting in the way back. For twenty minutes on the highway, she drifted in and out of my life. Through our gaze, we shared dreams of upgrading to the back.

When my sisters Gina and Patti got their driver's licenses, my brother Joe moved up to the front and I was upgraded to the back. The back was a comfortable chalet with some privacy still and gave me the chance to chime into conversations. I was able at least to be a backseat driver. I could say things like, "Where are we going?" and "What time is it?" When Joe got his own car, I moved up to the front seat. Wow. This was big. It felt like I was being born again at age eleven. Seeing the world in a whole new way. From the front. My mom and I would shoot the breeze. Stop in some place for a slice of pizza. Pop into CVS for some baking soda. No biggie. We're in the front.

In seventh grade I went on the Shrewsbury Middle School's annual trip to Washington DC. If I thought the front was eye-opening, a trip to another state with no parents was like diving into a pool full of ice water. We were chaperoned by our history teacher, Mr. Hutchinson. Every year he would cart a few busloads of students down to Washington DC by himself. For four days. And every year this trip was the same. I knew that because my sisters Gina and Patti had been on the trip and my brother Joe had too.

"Now here's what we're gonna do," Mr. Hutchinson

would shout in the classroom for months leading up to the trip. He repeated this over and over. "We're gonna load up these buses at seven a.m. And if you're not here, we leave without you."

Oh my God. They leave without us? Then what?

"Last year Jeremy Pile missed the bus. He spent the week picking weeds in his parents' lawn." There was always an example of what had happened to the last person who didn't follow these strict rules. Smart tactic.

"And then when we get to Washington DC, we meet up with Huntah." By the way, my sister Gina is eleven years older than I am. Different tour guide? Nope. Huntah. He goes by one name. "Huntah."

"And Hunter shows us around to all the monuments. All the museums. And we eat all our meals at Roy Rodgehs (Roy Rogers)." Mr. Hutchinson would say with a straight face to a bunch of impressionable children: "Washington DC has the best Roy Rodgehs." I later lived in Washington DC and discovered that the DC Roy Rogers really isn't that much different from any other Roy Rogers up and down the Jersey Turnpike, but at the time we took it as absolute fact. I actually remember repeating it to my parents: "They have the best Roy Rogers." My parents didn't even correct me. I think they just wanted me to stop talking.

We saw everything in Washington DC on that trip: Washington Monument, Jefferson Memorial, Vietnam Memorial, several Roy Rogers. The trip gave me a taste of a world outside of Shrewsbury.

. . .

When I finished college, I asked my mom for her car.

I had met with a comedy booker named Carl Hasselback. Carl's office smelled like pot and he had a Rolodex of the worst gigs in America. If you've ever driven by a motor lodge that inexplicably has the words "Comedy Night" illuminated on a sign out front, Carl probably booked it. I could call Carl more often than other bookers because he was usually so high that he wouldn't remember that I had called him five minutes before. He'd say, "Hey! Mike Birbaglio!" But Carl always took my calls, and I noticed that the first thing he asked was "Do you have a car?" Like he wasn't even looking for comedians. He was looking for guys with cars, just like the booker for Fat Tuesday. The primary component of a bad comedy gig is someone showing up. The words *someone* and *show up* are key. I knew I could do this. I certainly was someone. So I needed a car. To show up.

The only person I knew with an extra car was my mom. She was retiring her green '88 Volvo 740 station wagon. And when I say retiring, I mean the dealership offered her eight hundred dollars for it, and I begged her to just give it to me instead. This thing came loaded with the swing-down dog cage and perhaps some aging fruit in the way back, and years of wear and tear. My mom never took care of cars too well. In addition to her gas-and-brakes driving technique, she never got the oil changed. Ever. And she often drove the car on empty, which is like living in a house held up by hockey sticks. They might keep the house up for a while, but I wouldn't have any guests over for dinner. My mom tended to put things off. I may have picked up some of that trait along the way.

I performed in St. Louis, then Cleveland, then Pittsburgh, doing unpaid guest spots at comedy clubs where they might actually hire me in the future. On the trip from Cleveland to Pittsburgh, I noticed that the orange exclamation point popped up on the dashboard. I thought, *I'm sure that'll work itself out.*

I had already taken the car to the mechanic that week. After the gig in Pittsburgh, I drove home. It was about 1:00 a.m. and I couldn't imagine myself paying thirty-nine dollars for a hotel room after making no money all week and racking up more Capital One debt in gas and tolls. So I decided to make the drive, despite the glowing orange exclamation point on my dash. I've heard some people put electric tape over their orange exclamation point so they don't have to deal with it. Not me. I blocked it out in my brain. I scanned the radio for a caffeinated Eagles tune or perhaps some early Van Halen. And thirty minutes into my drive home, my mom's Volvo wagon starts going slower and then, eventually, stops.

I'm on the Pennsylvania Turnpike. It's 2:00 a.m. My cell phone is on low battery. I have used up the battery calling people to tell them how great my life is. I'm able to get off one call to Triple A (or as my mother calls it, "A, A, A.") before it dies. I'm sitting in my car in what is the smallest breakdown lane I've ever seen. It is probably about six feet wide, and trucks are whizzing past. And I'm praying that my car doesn't get hit. A tow truck arrives around 2:30 a.m.

A large, tough gentleman who looks like he might have killed some people in his prime starts attaching my mom's car to his tow truck. I didn't learn his name, but let's call him "Large."

Just as Large is about to attach the hook to my front axle, we hear the sound of an enormous truck engine. Large and

I look up and see an eighteen-wheeler about fifty yards away heading straight toward us. It's clear that the driver has fallen asleep, which is what I want to do, but now really isn't the time. I need to focus on staying alive.

So I take two steps off the road and plant my body against an embankment of dirt and dry grass like a white trash snow angel. And the tow truck driver bends his upper torso over the top of my car, his legs left dangling in the turnpike, trying to clutch the underbelly of the driver-side door with his toes. The sleepy truck veers over within inches of him, the truck driver *blares* his horn and veers back into the turnpike, now apparently well rested. Large and I have just escaped death. It is a bonding moment.

Large starts freaking out. He's like, "What the hell was that, man! I almost fucking died! I almost fucking died, man!" I shrug, just kind of repeating back what he said, but more quietly. "Yeah, what was that? We almost fucking died."

We get in the tow truck and he keeps going. He's like, "What the hell was that! We almost fucking died!" Minutes later, we're driving to the service station and he calls his wife and he's shouting into the phone: "I love you so bad, honey! I almost fucking died! Do you understand me!" I can faintly hear her return it back through the phone: "I love you so bad! You get home right now! Who's with you?"

Large hangs up the phone and pulls out a cigarette. He starts smoking fiendishly. And even though I don't smoke I ask for a cigarette. Now we're both chain-smoking. And I'm sitting there, smoking, thinking, We almost fucking died. *What the hell was that, man?*

We drop the car at the service station and he leaves me at

the worst motel I have ever stayed at. It's called The Sleep Inn, which is kind of opposite of how I feel because I'm thinking, *I gotta get the fuck out of here.* The "all-night receptionist clearly with a shotgun" doesn't do much to calm my nerves. I barely sleep. I just lie there, waiting for the service station next door to open up for business. The next morning, after seven hundred dollars in station wagon repairs, I drive my battered tank back to Brooklyn.

I had done the worst gigs, made no money, stayed at the worst hotel, and nearly died. I was actually feeling pretty good. There was some part of me that thought, *At least I'm in the way front.* I'm driving up the Jersey Turnpike and I spotted a Roy Rogers. I stopped and had breakfast. It was the best Roy Rogers.

THE DEAL

When I was fifteen, my father forced me to get a summer job. I was spending a lot of time around the house. Every day he'd look at me for a moment, sum me up, and then shout in another direction, "This kid needs some goddamn reality testing!" I'm not sure who he was talking to, but I definitely heard him. He had a point—I hadn't taken any steps toward becoming a professional break-dancer or a hip hop recording artist, so it's possible that I did need a push. My brother Joe got me my first summer job, at a restaurant on Cape Cod. He had worked there the summer before as a prep cook, shucking oysters and deveining shrimp. Fortunately they needed busboys the day I walked in, because Joe's job seemed kind of terrible.

I met Tyler, the manager, in the front entranceway of the restaurant and followed him back toward the kitchen. Walking into the kitchen of a big restaurant is kind of like going backstage at the circus. It's all lit with fluorescent lighting, it smells funny, and everyone seems to be yelling at each other, often in languages you're not hearing in the dining room.

Since I was Joe's brother, the fix was in. Tyler asked me one question during our interview. Had I ever been a busboy before?

Of course I had. Joe had told me to say this. He had explained that the paradox of working at a restaurant is that you have to have previous experience working at a restaurant. Even if you don't. Get it?

"Got it. So I lie?"

"Well, it's more like implying."

"What if he asks me follow-up questions?"

"He won't. He doesn't want to know the truth. He's just trying to cover his ass."

Tyler didn't ask any follow-up questions and I got the job. The first thing Tyler did was give me some advice. Gesturing to the cooks behind the line, he said, "You gotta stay out of these guys' way in the kitchen. Get in and out of here with your trays as quickly as possible, and do not talk to them unless you absolutely must."

And since the kitchen was like 150 degrees and full of angry cooks, I said, "No problem."

The only time I would be in the kitchen was to clear trays, and I will confess, I was one of the busboys who hid the beer bottles that only had a sip taken out of them. My busboy colleagues and I held these near-full green bottles up to the light like chemists, agreeing that the alcohol in the beer should kill any of the bacteria in the backwash. And I think we were right, because none of us died.

I learned a lot about restaurant hierarchy that first summer. Primarily that the cooks are the angriest, sweatiest, most-underpaid people in the restaurant business. These grizzled, Boston-accented guys worked long shifts in a 145-degree kitchen and I think some of them may have had the sneaking suspicion that fifteen-year-old busboys drinking backwash-laced Heinekens and eating wedding cake were making more money than them, and they weren't amused.

But for some reason, I still wanted to connect with the cooks. To befriend them like they were some crazy stray dogs that just needed a little understanding and attention. To let them know that "hey, this guy at the garbage can eating the virtually untouched scallops wrapped in bacon was a real person too."

One day the head cook, this guy named Dave Rubio, looked at me with his dead eyes and said, "How'd you get this job anyway?" This was my big chance to connect with my coworkers. It was almost like he'd invited me on a corporate retreat, except instead of trust exercises where we catch each other from falling from a forty-foot tree, we have a basic human conversation. I know it's not much, but at the time it was huge. I was *speaking* to the cook. The Nic Cage of the kitchen, a guy who knew how to do more than just carry trays or pour sixteen ounces of beer into a sixteen-ounce glass.

And I said, "My brother Joe worked here last summer."

And his eyes lit up. He goes, "*Joey Bag o' Donuts?* Your brother is Joey Bag o' Donuts?"

Now, what I should have said was "Why don't I ask him and get back to you? I know for sure his name is Joe."

What I did say was "Yeah."

Dave turned to the rest of the kitchen and shouted out, "Hey! Get this! This guy's Joey Bag o' Donuts' brother!"

This announcement was met by a chorus of approval, "All right!" "Yeah!" "Joe Bags' little brother! You're all right man!"

That day I went home and asked my brother, "Was your nickname at the restaurant Joey Bag o' Donuts?"

And Joe said, "No. That was this other guy. That guy was awesome."

For the rest of the summer, I had to live the lie that my brother was Joey Bag o' Donuts. All the cooks, with their eyes lit up like I had been accepted in the Lit-up Eyes Society, would look at me and say, "How's Joe Bags?"

And I'd say, *"He's great."*

One time one guy said, "Seriously, how much can Joe Bags drink?"

And I said, "So . . . much."

The whole summer I felt this pit of fear in my stomach that one day the actual Joe Bags would walk in the door to that kitchen and they'd all put me on their shoulders and say "Joe Bags, we've been hanging out with ya' brutha!" And Joe Bags would look at me and say, "That fag's not my brutha." And that's when they would drop me into a cauldron of New England clam chowder.

Upon moving to New York after graduation, I realized that I needed money to pay for frivolous things like rent and bags of noodles. For my college graduation, my family bought me a thousand dollars' worth of "Ask Jeeves" stock, which was immediately worth about three hundred and twenty dollars. I knew I had about six months to be successful. I lived for a month on my sister Gina's couch in Brooklyn. She had a small one-bedroom, but was willing to trade me pizza for doing her laundry.

I didn't have much luck getting stage time at comedy clubs,

despite some somewhat clever marketing tactics. When I called bookers, they would ask for "dupes" of my tape. In order to get club owners familiar with you, you were expected to provide a demo tape of your work. My sister Gina worked at HBO so all the dupes had HBO stickers on them. It was a bit misleading.

"This Birbiglia guy has an HBO special? Wait a minute— this was shot on a hi-8 in the back of a comedy club next to a tray of clinking glasses! What the hell kind of HBO special is that?"

Calling club bookers is kind of like telemarketing, except you never have to say, "Is your mom there?" But you follow similar principles. Never leave a message. Always try and get a live person on the phone, and try to keep the conversation going. "Oh, you don't want to book me this week? Okay, how about next week? Oh, you don't like me in general? Well, maybe I could interest you in some hair care products?"

Only one club booker actually took my calls. His name was Lucien Hold and he was the manager of the Comic Strip Live on the Upper East Side of Manhattan. Lucien was a New York comedy institution. He had been booking the club since the seventies and had supposedly given breaks to Jerry Seinfeld, Chris Rock, Eddie Murphy, and many others. He was a former ballet dancer who believed that comedy was an art form. He also believed in telling people exactly how he felt about their art, and he had a habit of talking at length. So not only would Lucien explain to you why he didn't find you talented, but he would do so *for a while*.

Apparently on one occasion Lucien was in his closet-sized office giving notes to a female comedian, who was slightly overweight, and he said to her, "You're overweight but it's not comical."

"Excuse me?" she said.

He said, "In other words, you're not sexy enough to interest people with your looks and not fat enough to be a sight gag."

She said, "Are you serious?"

Lucien said, "Oh yes. I'm not saying you can't be a comedian. I'm just saying you can't be a comedian at this club."

Lucien had some enemies.

But he was honest, and honesty was a quality that was hard to come by when I was cold-calling bookers. I respected honesty more than unreturned phone calls. The first time I performed for Lucien, he said, "You're a cross between Jim Gaffigan, Jeffrey Ross, and Todd Barry, and those guys already work the club, so I don't need you." Then he just waited for my reply. But I didn't really have one. I liked those comics too. So I just made something up: "But I'm young and I'll get better."

He thought about this and said, "That's true, but there are a lot of younger guys. I mean, it's not like you talk about particularly young topics."

I was stumped. I said, "I talk about the Teletubbies."

He said, "The Teletubbies are for babies. Infants. We don't serve infants."

I had found myself on the wrong side of a preposterous argument. I was somehow an advocate of infant drinking. Lucien decided not to "pass me" at the club. That was the term for being on the booking list. When you are "passed" you get a phone number to call and leave your weekly availability. I wasn't passed, but Lucien told me to come back in the fall.

• • •

This left me with a lot of time on my hands and no real prospects for work. My brother "Joe Bags" had moved to New York a few years before me and he had some ideas for me. He got me a job as a focus group participant. Well, sort of a job. It's kind of like jury duty, but instead of deciding the fate of some alleged murderer, you work with a team of equally broke New Yorkers to decide the fate of the newest Del Monte canned fruit cocktail recipe, which will be called either "Extra Cherries Jubilee," "The Cherry on Top Cocktail," or maybe even "The Very Cherry Explosion." Your opinion can change history. And you get paid.

The first focus group I participated in had candy and sandwiches and lemonade in the waiting room. It was fantastic. But I got a little suspicious. *Why are they being so nice? Sandwiches in New York cost eight or nine dollars. How did I stumble upon this sandwiches gold mine?*

After eating two or three of the sandwiches, I was ushered into a conference room and seated with ten other strangers and an overly enthusiastic moderator. The entire wall behind her was a one-way mirror, which she asked us to ignore, as if that were possible. It was easy to imagine the young ad agency hotshots and their clients back there, trying to guess how many of the free Hydrox chocolate cookies I could possibly stuff down my throat. The answer: many. But I was happy because I was making fifty dollars an hour to eat cookies and babble like a drunk person about fruit cocktail. I was winning.

Focus groups seemed pretty great. They were like taking college courses called "Introduction to Fruit Cocktail" and "Breakfast Sandwiches." And there's no homework, there's never going to be a test, and there are no wrong answers.

Sometimes my fellow focus room participants said things

about advertisements and products that blew my mind. I saw a flight attendant scream, "I can't stand all those goddamn cherries they put in those fruit cups!" I wanted to say, "Debbie, sit back and have a Hydrox cookie, you'll feel a lot better." Instead I just ate more Hydrox cookies. I may have even eaten some of her share.

But sometimes I was the idiot.

At one point I was at a focus group for Sam Adams beer, looking at and offering critiques for some new television ads. The ads were fine, and the moderator asked us what we thought of the beer, the Sam Adams brand, and Sam Adams the historical figure. And the young man on my left started talking about his impression of Sam Adams as an American patriot and Revolutionary War hero. And I have no idea why, but I tried to correct him. I jumped in and pointed out that Sam Adams wasn't a patriot or a revolutionary, he was just a guy who made beer, a brewer. Maybe I was trying to show off for the people behind the glass. I knew they were behind there, mocking his ignorance, and I suppose by jumping in I thought I could differentiate myself, you know, pile on the dumb guy. I had to let those people know I was not with this guy. I was my own man, a man with cookie crumbs stuck in my eyebrows. I have no idea what I was thinking. I found out later that Sam Adams was the cousin of John Adams and is generally considered one of the foremost leaders of the American Revolution. The point is, they gave me fifty dollars.

If I could do these every week, I thought, I'll be set. I'll be the king of fifty-dollar bills in envelopes! When someone asks me to pay for a check at a restaurant, I'll just ask, "How many fifty-dollar bills is that?" And then I'll pull out one of my fifty-dollar bill envelopes, and unleash one of my crisp cincuentas. But I had a hard time qualifying for focus groups every week. Sometimes I wouldn't fit the demographic they were searching for, so I learned to say whatever it took to qualify. Instead of truthful answers like, "No, I don't drive a Mitsubishi," "No, I don't frost the tips of my hair," and, "No, I don't supervise an office of ten or more employees," I opted for the "correct" answers, like "I drive a Mitsubishi Eclipse," "I always frost my tips," and "Of course, I manage our entire sales force on the Eastern seaboard." Oh, and I also said I *love* NASCAR. That was probably the biggest stretch.

CALLER: Mike, how many times a week would you say that you read NASCAR magazines? Zero to two, three to five, or six to seven days?

ME: Oh, definitely six to seven days a week, definitely.

CALLER: Great. And how many times a week do you email your friends about NASCAR races: zero to four, five to twelve, or, more than twelve times per week?

ME: More than twelve.

The ad agencies and their clients try to cover their asses and weed out the fakers. They can't have these focus groups be total catastrophes, so they try to nail you with the last question. Fortunately, the caller is paid by how quickly she can fill up these focus groups, so she's on your side.

CALLER: And finally, could you name your three favorite NASCAR drivers?

And you'd think, for a guy who reads NASCAR magazines six or seven days a week and emails his friends constantly about their progress and outcomes, this wouldn't be too difficult a question, but somehow, I still struggled.

ME: Sure, sure . . . ok, hmmm . . . is there a Dale?
CALLER: Dale Earnhardt Jr?
ME: Yes, him. And that guy Ricky, with the glasses and the hat, he drives really fast.
CALLER: You mean Ricky Rudd?
ME: Yes, Ricky Rudd, and of course, everyone's favorite, Dick Trickle. He's my third favorite.
CALLER: (pause) Uh, he retired a long time ago. Can we just say Jeff Gordon?
ME: Oh yes, I love him too. Jeff is great. Super fast racer.

So I qualified. And by this point in the call, I figured out that the focus group is going to be about some sort of NASCAR-themed technology, probably a website. So I thought, *Oh, I'll hang back in this focus group, and just focus on eating cookies.* But when I arrived for the group, I looked around the room and there are all these other young guys who had also clearly lied their way into this focus group, and our grossly uninformed discussion about NASCAR began.

Somebody asked if NASCAR is the one with the low-slung pointy cars or the big road-type cars. There may be no such thing as a dumb question, but if you're supposed to be a huge NASCAR fan, that is a dumb question. As I looked around the room at the faces of the other nervous Hydrox cookie eaters, it

hit me, *I know more about NASCAR than most of these people.*
The moderator proceeded to show us this really elaborate website all about NASCAR and NASCAR chat rooms and NAS-
CAR stats, and then this other guy suggested that they build
a website like this around baseball, because that's *his* favorite
sport. At this point everyone in the room, including the moderator, turned to this guy with this look, like, *Are you stupid?*
They are giving us fifty-dollar bills and Hydrox cookies to pretend
we like NASCAR. You will not ruin this for all of us. Your favorite
sport is NASCAR.

We all started to catch heat from the moderator. She was
looking around at us like, *None of you losers watch NASCAR, do*
you? But she couldn't say it, because then the jig would have really been up. I felt for her. Who were these losers who had lied
to this company so they could make some extra cash?

I looked in the one-way mirror and saw my answer.

With nothing going on in New York and my couch welcome
at Gina's wearing thin, I moved back home with my parents. It
was more or less a full-time job in tech support and lawn care
in exchange for being able to sleep in my childhood bed.

I spent my days roving the Internet on my parents' computer for contests I could enter, kind of like the character Lazlo
in the movie *Real Genius.* But while Lazlo's strategy had to do
with any contest, mine was comedy contests. In retrospect this
strategy was kind of insane, it was like I thought, *I just need*
to win a contest for my career to take off. Boy, I sure hope such a
contest exists!

Fortunately, such a contest did exist. Comedy Central was holding a "Laugh Riots" standup comedy competition in major cities nationwide. The winners of these regional contests would compete in Los Angeles for a spot on a Comedy Central standup show called *Premium Blend*. When I told my dad that I was accepted into the semifinals, he asked me what it paid, and I said, "It only pays if you win. Because it's a contest." And he said, "Are you going to get a job winning contests?"

He had a point, and I didn't win, but one of the judges named Michelle from Comedy Central told me I was "kind of funny" and gave me her card. I told her I'd be back in New York soon and I'd call her when I got there. I wasn't planning to move back to New York, but now that I had this business card, it seemed like a worthwhile life choice. *I'm kind of funny!*

I found an apartment in New York with dirt-cheap rent and at night I would go to comedy clubs and try to just "be around." That was advice I was given. Just "be around." I was around at the Comic Strip one night when Lucien said to me, "Mike, I'm not passing you at the club but I was asked to put some young comics on a showcase for Adam Sandler's production company. Maybe you could do some of your Teletubbies material." That Saturday night I killed in front of a hot 8:00 p.m. crowd. I had to. It was my only chance. Lucien said, "Audiences seem to like you. Why don't you call the club with your availability?"

Then he looked over at his assistant Maria and said, "Will you write down the phone number for Mike?" That meant I could do one spot a week at the club and that if I hung out for the whole night on standby I might perform on "late night," which meant that if there was even one last pathetic audience member left after a four-hour show who was still willing to order a drink, I would go on. I was there every night. Maria wrote the number down on a Comic Strip business card and I still remember it. 212-496-1424. It was one of the only numbers I called for the next six months.

I was getting one spot a week at the Comic Strip, which paid ten dollars, so I needed another $460 a month to pay my rent. I needed a plan.

I asked my struggling actor friends if they had any tips for making cash, and my friend Chris said, "Call this number and ask for Diane. Tell her that I sent you." So I called the number and a cheery voice answered: "This is the Laurie Group!" It was the kind of voice that you imagine stewardesses in the seventies had and I thought, *How come no one pretends to be that happy anymore?*

I asked for Diane and she said, *"Absolutely!"* This was going to be much easier than I thought. Maybe she'll bring me a soft drink and a warm towel. I spoke to Diane and she couldn't have been more thrilled to get my call. She *loved* Chris, which was strong language, because I wasn't even sure *I* loved Chris. I mean I loved Chris like Jesus loves *all*, but I didn't love him more than *others*. I told her that I had recently graduated from college and was looking for a job.

She said, *"Fantastic!"* It was the best news she had heard all day: *I had graduated from college!*

Diane invited me to come in for an interview the next day. In the waiting room, I read the Laurie Group literature and discovered that the Laurie Group had originally been an all-women's temp agency. They called their temps "Laurie Girls." Just recently they had started using some guys. So they were "Laurie Girls and some guys." Diane called me in for the interview and it went as well as the phone conversation. Before I left, they asked me to take a typing test. Now, typing is certainly not my forte. Over the years I had flirted with Mavis Beacon but we'd never gone all the way. When I only scored about forty-two words per minute, they weren't thrilled with my score, but it was enough. They said they had an assignment for me the next day. It only paid eleven dollars an hour but it would get my foot in the door. I felt like Tom Hanks's character in *Big*.

"Eleven dollars an hour?"

I had gotten my first real-world job. I was a Laurie Girl (and some guys.)

I showed up to an advertising firm the next day. The offices were in a forty-five-story building and I was given a desk in the basement.

How about floor two? Or three? Anything near the commissary? No.

Basement. No windows. Not many people, really. But I had an overseer who showed me how to do data entry. Data entry is a fascinating job where you . . . type . . . in . . . data . . . that's been . . . written on something else. You can press tab and jump from field to field, and you need to remember to capitalize proper nouns like people's names and their streets. The first ten minutes of data entry fly by, because you're really getting the hang of it. The remaining seven hours and fifty minutes go a lot more slowly, because you glance at the clock after you finish every entry.

Data entry is the white-collar equivalent of potato peeling. "Oh, you finished peeling all those potatoes? Well super, because we have a couple hundred more sacks of potatoes!"

I fell asleep with such regularity at this job that I developed a strategy for falling asleep while sitting up in the typing position. It was the closest my life had come to *Ferris Bueller's Day Off,* and it worked. No one ever caught me sleeping. But one day I had been sleeping for a whole hour. I had slept so long that when I woke up I needed to surf the web as a stimulant to get riled up for some more hard-core data entry action. And as I was surfing the web, my overseer sneaked up behind me, looked at my screen, and said, "I caught ya! You're checking your email." I thought, *You should have been here five minutes ago when I was unconscious. That would have been far more exciting.*

I thought that would be the end of my Laurie Girl days, but it wasn't. They called me the next week with a new job. A better job. An administrative assistant at a women's magazine that paid fifteen dollars an hour. It was a three-day stint with potential for more if I did well. I went in and did my first two days, and I rarely saw my boss but I answered her phone and did anything else anybody asked me to.

The night before my third day, I had been up doing the late night show at the Comic Strip, which started around 1:00 a.m. and went until about 2:00 or 2:30. After that, I did some more shows at other smaller venues. Starting out as a comic in New York City, it's not unusual to get a five-minute slot at three in the morning performing in front of three other people, who themselves are waiting to do their own five-minute slot. These aren't at comedy clubs; they're in hotel lobbies or in dark, strange apartments that have been filled with long wooden benches and converted to performance spaces. It was kind of like I was living the life of a superhero: by day I was an administrative assistant, and by night I was an insomniac with five minutes of comedy.

So after these shows I got back to my apartment in Astoria, Queens, around 3:30 a.m. and don't recall anything else until looking at my clock at 11:15 a.m. And I was three hours late for my job at the women's magazine. I scrambled to the R line on the subway and by the time I got to the office it was almost noon. *Maybe no one had noticed?*

There was a woman working at the desk next to me, and she solemnly said, "Hey Mike, you're supposed to call your temp agency."

I said, "Okay," and picked up the phone and called Diane.

"Hey Mike! They're not going to need you today, so just fill out a timecard for your travel time to and from your apartment and we'll get you paid for that."

I felt a little bad. I looked over at my boss's closed door and then I whispered to the woman who sat next to me, "Should I pop in her office and apologize?"

She looked at me like I had just asked her, "Is a fork the thing with the four sharp pointy things, or is that the spoon?"

She said, "Mike, I don't think you want to go in there."

I said, "Is it because I was so late?"

She said, "She didn't like you before you were late. There was a whole list of things you didn't do."

As it turns out, there was an actual list. Because this woman who sat next to me pulled it out and started reading it. Things like opening and sorting the boss's mail, getting her lunch, and a bunch of other very specific tasks. I was so much worse an employee than I ever could have imagined and on top of that, I didn't even show up. On my way out, my cubicle neighbor said, "You know, Mike, we do like you. It would be great if you were here but you're not." She was right.

My agent Marcy called and said in her unusually high-pitched voice, "You need to fly to Hollywood immediately! Immediately!!"

I had just returned from the Montreal Comedy Festival where I had performed in the "New Faces of Comedy" category.

"I've set up some meetings for you."

"Uh . . . okay." I said. "What are these meetings about?"

"We gotta get you a deal!"

"What kind of deal?"

"A sitcom deal!"

Marcy told me stories about Ray Romano and then a bunch of people I had never heard of who got deals after this festival for ridiculous sums of money. This was a perfect situation. Someone was going to give me a lot of money and I needed a lot of money. At this point, my bank balance was in parentheses, which means, "Let's say you had money, it *might* be this much money, but since you don't, you owe us this much money." If I could get a deal, I could stop temping.

I said, "Count me in, Marcy! Let's go get a deal!"

I didn't even like sitcoms. I didn't want to be on a sitcom. What I wanted to be was a traveling comedian. But I thought, *This will be the thing that will get my parents off my back!*

My parents had been urging me to get out of comedy and make a real living ever since I announced my chosen "profession." The first time I told my father I was performing at comedy clubs he said, "Comedy clubs? What do they do? Strip? You can't make a living doing that! *You need some god-damn reality testing!!"*

He had a point. Not about the stripping, but about the career choice. The overwhelming majority of comics lose money each time they perform. By the time you include your many expenses (gas, tolls, rental cars, Funyuns), the seventy-five-dollar gig fee disappears fast.

It's 11:30 p.m. and I get off the phone with Marcy and I book the first flight I can to Los Angeles. For the next few days, I do what everyone in Hollywood does instead of their job: I take meetings.

I'm taking meetings with people who are theoretically going to give me a deal. I have no idea what I am doing. I later found out that neither did Marcy. She would call these production companies or networks I was meeting with and say, "Mike needs a deal!" Which, I think, is the opposite of how you get a deal. You have to pretend you have all kinds of deals about to happen. Like you're gonna pass out if you get handed one more deal. You can't tell them you need a deal. I thought Marcy and I had a kind of secret code language. Nope, that was our strategy: *Mike needs a deal.*

For six days I stayed on my friend Adam's couch and he chauffeured me around town. I couldn't get a rental car because they don't accept parentheses. He would drive me from meeting to meeting. Adam is gay, in the stereotypical way where he criticizes the way I dress and look and act. He's like Perez Hilton except he's willing to rip apart your appearance even if you're not famous. I would go to these meetings, and it would go okay. Then I'd come out to the car and Adam would say, "You look fat in that shirt."

I'd be like, "Well, thank you. I was feeling pretty good a second ago, but I had been meaning to have my self-esteem knocked down to negative a thousand."

Executives call these "general meetings" though they really ought to call them "meaningless events that make it seem like I shouldn't lose my job, which I should." These are meetings with networks and companies who have quirky names like Pinball Machine Productions or serious names like Serious Productions. You know—those companies that have their names on the end of TV shows but you don't know what the hell they do. Well, I'll tell you what they do. They have "general meetings." These meetings are about thirty to sixty minutes long and they're kind of like a speed date.

"What do you do? How'd you get started?"

The way to look cool in these meetings is to act like you have no idea why you're there or why you'd ever want to talk about show business. You say stuff like, "Isn't it crazy that polar bears can hear their prey from thirty miles away?"

And they say, "Mike Birbiglia is so *interesting*. He doesn't care about show business at all!"

And then immediately after the meeting my agent Marcy would call and say, "Mike needs a deal!"

I would go into these meetings and the people in the meetings would insist that I was going to get a deal. They'd say things like, "You're definitely going to get a deal." And, "You don't have a deal? You will." Then they'd wink like they knew something I didn't. After a few days of this, I started to believe it. I was calling everyone I knew. I was like, "I'm about to get a sitcom deal." I think "about to" are two of the most danger-ous words in the English language. Never trust people who say things like "I'm about to" or "Because I'm high."

At this point, I'm calling my parents, my brother Joe, my friends from college. "You were wrong about me! I'm gonna get a deal! I'm gonna have my own sitcom! I'm about to date Heather Locklear!"

Even my dad, always skeptical, took note: "How much do they give you for these deals?"

I said, "I think like a hundred thousand dollars."

My dad said, "Well, I guess *I'm* in the wrong profession."

I said, "Yeah, I know." And I thought, *Who needs some reality testing now?*

A few days later I fly home, and as I'm sitting on the plane it's occurring to me that I don't have a deal. I think, *What about my deal? That lady from Siamese Twins Entertainment told me that I was going to get a deal! The guy from Choco-Taco Productions told me I was a genius, and should maybe co-host some kind of polar bear animated feature thing!*

I land in New York and check my messages.

No messages.

I call Marcy.

"Hey . . . what's up with the deal?"

Marcy says, "It doesn't look like it's going to happen. No one's getting deals this year."

I found out later that this is what they tell people who don't get deals, that no one got a deal. But they did. Some people did. Just not me.

I get back to my tiny apartment and I look at my paren-theses balance and I feel so tricked. I was made to believe that my life was going to be fixed and it wasn't. I'm still the same loser who had flown to Los Angeles on my sister's frequent flier miles just six days before. It was my first brush with a business full of fast talkers. They convinced me that my life was going to be changed, and it wasn't. I think this is the reality my dad had warned me about.

I CAN'T STOP!

I was the youngest of four kids, so really anytime anyone was willing to talk to me or spend any time with me at all, I would gladly accept. My brother took advantage of this, and so when I was three, I became Joe's personal soccer goalie.

I got to be pretty good. I was never a natural athlete, but I developed an uncanny ability to dive headfirst at soccer balls. "You gotta throw your body at the ball," Joe would say. And I would. I thought, *All you got to do to win is throw your body at the ball.*

A few years later my diving-headfirst-at-balls technique paid off when I was selected as the starting goalie for Shrewsbury's prestigious traveling soccer team.

During the game, in Oxford, Massachusetts, I went head-to-head with an Oxford forward in what's called a 50–50 ball, meaning we each had a 50–50 chance of getting to it. I dove headfirst and got to the ball.

That was the good part.

The bad part was that when the other team's player arrived at my head, he decided, since there was no longer a ball available, to kick my head with the same velocity that he would have used to kick the ball.

Let me rephrase that: an eleven-year-old kid kicked my head as though it were a soccer ball that needed kicking as hard as humanly possible. I don't remember anything after that, but here's what I'm told happened next:

1. The referee blew the whistle and a bunch of players and coaches ran over to me, shouting, "Are you okay? Are you okay?" I jumped right up and said, "I'm great! I'm fine!" They said, "Are you sure?" I said, "Yeah! I'm good!"

2. The game continued.

3. About five minutes later, I started walking aimlessly off the field, oblivious to the game in which I was participating. I recognized one person: Tom Bachmann, my defenseman and the coach's son. "Tom . . . " Tom looked over at me. I was no longer on the field. I was somewhere between the field and a concession stand nearby. Tom said, "Mike, what's going on?" I said, "Tom, what are we *doing*?" Tom said, "Mike, we're playing a soccer game." I said, "Tom . . . I think I need to talk to my dad."

The coaches ran over, as did my dad. They pulled me out of the game and put in another goalie named Jim, who was immediately scored on four or five times. Apparently he did not have the proper throw-your-body-at-the-ball mentality that the position required. We lost pretty badly. I drove home with my dad, disoriented. They were careful to make sure I didn't go to sleep because of that whole thing with concussions and sleeping and dying. And I never played goalie again. But I used that aggression elsewhere.

• • •

When you're self-employed, you're your own boss. You're also your own employee. You're also your own tech support. And your own finance department. All those jobs can make one person a little crazy.

I was living in Astoria, Queens, temping during the day and performing in New York City or driving to nearby cities at night. I was always on, and when I was off, I was still on, because the on/off switch wasn't working too well. It's actually never worked too well. I've always envied those people who have this very nuanced control over their own energy. People who can work in low gear for a few hours, take the night off and relax, and put it in high gear in the morning, only to put it into low gear for the afternoon again. I don't have that. I'm a manic worker and manic sleeper. I've always crashed into sleep versus slowly easing into it. I'm a compulsive everything.

I didn't go into show business with the intention of performing in hundreds of cafeterias, auditoriums, and multipurpose centers at colleges across the country. But in 2002, about a year into my move to New York, I was introduced to Jill McGee, who books college gigs exclusively and submits comedians to the National Association for Campus Activities (NACA) conferences. These are held seven times a year in hotel conference centers across America and they consist of live shows and then conference room "marketplaces" filled with booths where live comedy is just one of the offerings. At a regional NACA in Reno, I walked around to see some of the other booths. There was Karges the Mentalist, who bends not only spoons but also forks. There was Sailesh, the "World's Best Uncensored Hypnotist." There were lecture events like Gail Hand's lecture "The

Power of Laughter." *Gail and I could be a duo,* I thought. *I could make the audiences laugh and then she could explain why they were laughing.* Perhaps my favorite booth was "The Mystical Arts of Tibet," where students are encouraged to participate in some kind of eastern philosophy equivalent of Lite-Brite. All the booths tended to have some kind of gimmick. They hook you with something like free cookies—which worked on me. Another popular gimmick was the use of an air-filled fat suit and huge boxing gloves. One booth just had a gigantic chair, which students would sit on and have their photos taken, in an effort to appear tiny. I asked them what they sold and they said, "This *is* what we sell."

The reason this wide variety of talented people is assembled in one place is that college activity booking is a pretty lucrative industry. Because the number of drinking-related deaths has skyrocketed in recent years, college administrations have no choice but to book as many non-drinking-related activities as possible. Drinking really is an issue. When I performed in the multipurpose center at Penn State, they were celebrating a made-up holiday called "State Patty's Day." Apparently Saint Patrick's Day usually falls during spring break, and the students at Penn State felt totally ripped off by this gross calendar injustice. So, not wanting to miss out on a holiday dedicated to binge drinking, they invented another one. Penn State students are nothing if not inventive (and drunk).

However, one year St. Patrick's Day *didn't fall* during their spring break, so when I arrived on campus to perform, they were celebrating both State Patty's Day and Saint Paddy's Day. I knew this fake holiday should be red-flagged when I picked up the college newspaper and read the headline

I CAN'T STOP!

"Victim Takes Partial Blame." I thought, *Are the Penn State headline writers also drinking? Because that headline seems like it was written by someone who had just knocked down several mojitos.*

Intrigued by the slurred headline, I continued. The story covered a widely discussed event on campus in which a drunk driver hit a drunk walker. I thought, *Hey, maybe these people shouldn't be making up holidays to drink more. Maybe if they drank less they might be able to title their newspaper articles more specifically.* For example, I would title this last article "Drunk Driver Hits Drunk Walker Drunkety-Drunk I'm So Drunk."

With all this drunkenness, these colleges needed to book mentalists, lecturers, and, sometimes, me.

I've performed at Maryland, Merrimack, Marymount, Marietta, William & Mary, Mary Washington, George Washington, and Georgetown.

I've played the Big East, the Pac-10, and the PacWest.

I've played Washington, Western Washington, and Eastern Washington.

I've played orientations, homecomings, Halloweens, senior balls, frat parties, student centers, common rooms, cafeterias, chapels, hockey rinks, basketball arenas, and the Sun Dome.

I've played UC Berkeley, UC Riverside, UCLA, SUNY Cobleskill, SUNY Binghamton, and SUNY Albany.

Let's see . . . Chapman, Curry, Bowdoin, Bates, Bentley, Bradley, Babson . . .

Of course there was Middle Tennessee State. And yes, I said *Middle*. And they do get offended if you mix them up with Tennessee State. Trust me.

And then there's Wisconsin. Ah, Wisconsin. I played UW–Stevens Point, UW–Whitewater, UW–Marinette, UW–Superior, UW–River Falls, UW–Stout, UW–Eau Claire. I played Carthage. All of these schools fed me cheese.

I played Anchorage and Fairbanks. I saw the aurora borealis and swam in the naturally occurring hot springs. That was nice.

I played DePaul, DePauw, Defiance, and Delaware . . .

I did Penn College, Penn State, UPenn, Penn State Behrend, and Alvernia College, which is in Pennsylvania but doesn't have a catchy name.

I've played St. Rose, St. Mary's, College of the Assumption, Salve Regina, Notre Dame . . .

I played Michigan, Michigan State, Central Michigan, Northern Michigan.

I did shows at West Virginia Tech, Texas Tech, Illinois Tech.

I did BU, CU, NYU.

I played Johnson & Wales (twice) where some people major in "pastry." The food in the cafeteria was terrible.

I did shows at Harvard, Princeton, Yale, and Columbia.

Middlebury, Monmouth, Rider, Ripon, Case Western, Northwestern, and Norwich University, which is a private military college in Vermont.

These are just a few.

Colleges tend to be an uphill battle for the performer. I have often been placed, for example, in the lunchroom, during lunch. These shows are called "nooners." One time I did a nooner at Rhode Island College and it got reviewed in the school paper. AJ Paglia wrote, "There were enough stand-up comedian mistakes of that day to fill the Grand Canyon, and if he said, 'No one's laughing' one more time, he would have won a free toaster. At one point, he began telling a bit about cell phones, and then paused, ineptly looked at the crowd, and then began a different bit. He forgot his joke!"

Looking back, I can't remember much about this show, but I believe AJ, especially that confusing analogy about the Grand Canyon. My depth of failure at that show was as deep as a tourist attraction that advertises deepness. I didn't even realize I was in contention for a toaster, but had I known, I would have pulled out my toaster-centric material. And if I had really wanted a toaster, I could have just stolen one. I was in the cafeteria. And frankly, I don't see what's wrong with repeatedly saying, "No one's laughing." It's simply my way of pointing out where people might laugh if they think what I've said is funny. I was being helpful. Besides, without the "No one's laughing" repetition, my set would have really been too short. And no one, with the exception of AJ Paglia, would have wanted that.

AJ's article concluded by saying that "Birbiglia had a very weak, pitiful character to him," which I feel crosses a certain line of meanness. To criticize my signature Grand Canyon–style of comedy is one thing, but my character? That feels personal. And I definitely felt hurt when this came to me via Google alert at two-thirty in the morning. *I do have a pitiful character,* I thought, and *Why am I awake?*

Sometimes colleges booked me in their finest venue on campus and that would be problematic as well, but for different reasons. Then it would be an issue because the students were sometimes disappointed to learn I was their main event for the semester. I was once asked to perform at Yale University in the prestigious Woolsey Hall. Unfortunately, the previous year they'd had Lewis Black, which means that my show probably signaled some kind of budget cut. A Google alert directed me to a *Yale Daily News* article:

> Stand-up comedian Mike Birbiglia will perform at this year's Fall Show. Students had mixed reactions to the news of this year's performer, as many students said they were not familiar with Birbiglia.

At first I thought, thanks *Yale Daily News*! As though my self-esteem isn't low enough, you've invited me to your school and now there's an article dedicated to the fact that you've never heard of me. It's like asking a girl to the prom and then, when she says yes, saying to her, "You see, last year my date was way hotter than you, but she graduated, and so I figured, why the hell don't I ask you? Perhaps I've never heard of you, but that shouldn't matter, right?"

I thought, surely there must be *someone* who's heard of me. Otherwise why would they have invited me? Then I read, "Dan Nagler, class of 2008, said he has never heard of the comedian and is unsure whether he will attend the show. '[I'm] not disappointed necessarily,' he said. 'Just because I don't know him doesn't mean he's not awesome.'"

Phew, I thought. Dan may not be attending the show but at least he's not ruling out the possibility of me being awesome. Of course, it's hard to be awesome when no one attends your show, so there's kind of a catch-22 there. As I read further, there was a ray of hope: "Though he had never heard of Birbiglia, Austin Shiner, '11, said he will likely attend. But a higher-profile comedian would make for a more exciting event. 'I suppose at the end of the day, I think Robin Williams when he's on his game is just about unbeatable,' Shiner said. 'If they had found a way to get Robin Williams to come, it would have been unbelievable.'" Finally, I thought, a voice of reason. Austin Shiner has this *Bill and Ted*–style idea about taking a time machine back to 1979 and booking Robin Williams in his prime. While we're at it, why don't we have Jimi Hendrix open the show and just play the hits? Now that we're brainstorming, is FDR available to speak at graduation? The article ends with a quote from Maddy Blount, '08, saying she did not know of Birbiglia but is glad that "the Fall Show will actually take place during the fall this year." Glad to be of some help, Maddy. If there's one thing Mike Birbiglia knows, it's when fall is. September, October, November, right? Nice.

When I received this Google alert at 1:41 a.m., I sent a letter to the *Yale Daily News*. I wrote, "I'm still planning to come to your school and I'm going to put on the best show I can. A great man once said, 'Just because you don't know who I am doesn't mean I'm not awesome.' I'm trying to stay positive. After all, my first choice was to perform at Harvard. You were my safety school."

One day Jill called and asked if I was willing to perform at five colleges in four days in Oregon and Washington State. It was short notice because one of her other comedians had to cancel. Perfect. I wasn't the colleges' *first* choice. But given the choice of me or no show at all, I had triumphed over nothing.

"Five in four days is a lot, right?"

"Two of them are nooners."

"Right."

"It shouldn't be a big deal. Jump on a plane. Knock out some shows. Fly home."

This is the kind of language people use when they want you to forget about the extreme strain you're about to put on your body. "Jump on a plane." "Knock out" some shows. No mention of the "drive your ass off eleven hundred miles until you're almost asleep at the wheel" or "cram yourself into a seat with no leg room and endure six and a half hours next to a one-and-a-half-sized person who smells likes olives to a gig no one really wants you at." I looked at my bank account that was in parentheses and said, "Sure."

A few days later I wake up at 4:30 a.m. to jump on a plane, which is that part of the morning before the earth even exists. Before they've even programmed the Matrix. You walk out of your apartment and the road isn't even there. You walk out of your house, and there's just a guy with a laptop who yells, "We need a road, stat!" "How 'bout a building, Tank!"

I get a cab to the Newark airport. And I get my ticket. I hand it to the security lady. And she looks at my ticket and she says, "Well, this gate is completely wrong." I guess they changed the gate. The way she says it is like I was involved in the gate selection process. Like I didn't like the gate that was printed on my ticket, so I photoshopped my favorite gate onto the ticket and printed it myself. Like I took one look and said, "B twenty-two, I don't think so." No, I was not involved in the process. I was not even cc'd. So she says, "You need to take a tram to another terminal, and I suggest you run."

So I run.

There's nothing worse than being late for a flight because you're running with your roller suitcase and roller suitcases do not enjoy running.

They're like, "I don't want to run! I have wheels!"

And you're like, "Listen, roller suitcase, I'm not good at running either, but I tell you what, when we get to the hotel, I'll walk you in circles for a few hours."

I get to the tram area. Fortunately, they have a nice little thing where a sign says how many minutes until the next tram arrives. The sign says, "0 minutes." For a moment, I'm excited. I think, *Zero minutes! That's exactly how long I want to wait.* But there's no tram. It already drove away. Then the sign changes to "10 minutes."

I eventually reach the gate. And I'm sitting at the gate, and I fall asleep. I wake up to the sound of the gate door closing.

I jump out of my chair, but there's no one around.

They've closed the door, but I'm not on the fun side, with the airplanes and the pilot. On my side, it's just me and the Cinnabon lady, and the Cinnabon lady is not very well connected in the airline community. I ask, "Do you know the people who can open the door?"

And she says, "I just know the white stuff goes on the Cinnabon."

So here I am, I'm on the sad side of the door. I'm on the side with me and the Cinnabon lady, which normally I'd be very excited about. I'm a big fan of pastries the size of a baby that contain enough calories for a year. That seems like an effective use of time.

At that point I walk over and I start banging on the large window like in a romantic comedy. I think of yelling, "Stop the plane, Drew Barrymore's character!"

I do not make that flight.

So I'm on standby for the 10:00 a.m., which gets me into Seattle by 4:00 p.m., and I drive two and a half hours upstate to Bellingham, to Whatcom Community College, which is 106 miles. (Or according to Mapquest, up to two hours and thirty minutes in traffic. *Bingo, Mapquest!*) By the time I arrive, it's almost 7:00. The show starts at 7:30. I walk onto a recently built stage in the student center and pretend I'm not tired for about an hour. It's a very small crowd. Crowd? Well, about thirty people. At community colleges, since most students commute, they often bring comedians to try to bring people together. That night, they stayed apart. I was no help.

The next day I'm supposed to do the nooner, but I'm technically booked for 11:00 a.m., and it's about two hours away in Tacoma, so I think it's wiser to drive there that night. I start driving at 10:00 p.m., though it feels about 5:00 a.m. in terms of my emotional stability. I have no energy, but I think about the six months of rent this trip will take care of. *All I have to do is live through it,* I think.

The nooner is worse than I could have imagined. I have actually been booked to perform during a study hall. I'm performing. They're studying. *Who thought of this?* I wonder on stage, sometimes aloud, hoping there are no reviewers ready with their notebooks to crucify me with my own self-deprecating words. I don't know who to feel sorrier for: me or the people trying to study. There are like fifteen people trying to study biology and I'm in their face shouting, "The thing about panda bears is they look like each other!" I try to think up material that might apply to the subjects they are studying. *How many mitochondria does it take to power a cell? One. Because mitochondria are the powerhouse of the cell.* Not ready for prime time, that one. Afterward, I go to a local restaurant and drown my sorrows in an ice cream pie shaped like a baked potato. I know it's not healthy, but at least it's shaped like a vegetable.

I head for school three, Columbia Basin College. They have me hosting a lip-synch contest—which is not a format that I'm a fan of. And neither are the students. There are only two entries, and the director of student activities is furious. When she gets up to introduce me, she says, "In the past we've had fifteen or twenty entries and this year there were two. And we don't have to have this contest if you don't want to have it, because I'm not doing this for me. I'm doing this for you. And now the comedian, Mike Birbiglia!" And then I jog onstage and say, "Y'all ready to lip-synch? I can't hear you!" That was my lip-synch joke.

I'm driving to school four. At this point, I'm driving through the night through the Cascade Mountains to get to another nooner the next day and one final show the next night. About halfway through the mountains my gas tank is on empty and so I do what any logical person would.

I drive faster. That way I can avoid the suspense of running out of gas and just cut to that desperate standing-on-the-side-of-the-road thing.

It's late at night and there are very few streetlights. The road is windy and I've been on my phone talking to my sister Patti. So now that I might actually need my phone, it's dead. At this point I'm thinking only the darkest of thoughts. *I will be stranded in the mountains. It's freezing. I'll die. At the very least, I won't get to the nooner that's going to pay my rent for April.*

So I'm driving like a hundred miles an hour over a mountain and I'm making all these resolutions with myself, like, *If I get to a gas station, I am going to donate all of my clothing to the tsunami fund and I'm going to eat only vegetables.* Eventually I get to a gas station and I think, *Forget that plan. I'd like a full tank of gas and some Funyuns.* It's amazing how quickly your thoughts can go from *I think I'm gonna die* to *I think I'd like fake onion rings.*

School four is easy. People show up. They eat hot dogs and cotton candy in some kind of carnival-themed student center event that I don't even bother asking about, but it's fine. On to school five and then fly home.

School five is in Walla Walla, Washington. They booked me to perform in the center of the gymnasium during an all-night "Walkathon for Lupus." When I arrive the young man who booked me looks at me with a straight face and says, "I know it's not ideal." And he's right, because I have to hold a microphone and kind of oscillate like a desk fan that blows jokes. All night these participants walk around the track and sort of glance uncomfortably at me as they pass. It's like having a steady stream of people steadily walk out of my show, and then return, not miraculously, just a few minutes later on the other side of the track. It's not ideal. As ideal as it might sound, I can assure you it is not. But I am not going to take the fall for the tepid response I receive at this show. If you're walking around an indoor track for seven hours to raise money for charity, the last thing you want to see is me in the middle, chasing you with a microphone and yelling about the Teletubbies. The first thing you want to see is a cup of water, maybe some orange slices.

I have nothing left. I have made my rent. I return to the La Quinta Inn where the students booked me. It's 1:00 a.m. I'm completely exhausted. But I'm not going to sleep. I have one more thing to do. I have to check my email to see if any more gigs like this have come through. Because when you're self-employed, email becomes a sort of slot machine.

You log on to Yahoo with the thought, *What am I doing next week?*

Oh. Nothing.

Refresh . . .

Nothing.

I fall asleep with the laptop in my hands.

MY HERO

When I was in college my sister Gina had a job at HBO, and she would send me the latest comedy specials of comedians like Mitch Hedberg, Chris Rock, and Dave Attell. They were comics' comics. Guys whose comedy was so good they were above comparison, guys who I wanted to be.

Mitch was my favorite of these comics. He defied standup comedy convention entirely. His style was defined by his shyness offstage. Instead of trying to be something he wasn't and project confidence, he was vulnerable in his delivery. He'd look at the floor or even at the back wall away from the crowd and deliver lines like, "I wrote a letter to my Dad. I wrote, *I really enjoy being here,* but I accidentally wrote *rarely* instead of *really.* But I still wanted to use it, so I wrote, *I rarely drive steamboats, Dad—there's a lot of stuff you don't know about me. Quit trying to act like I'm a steamboat operator.* This letter took a harsh turn right away."

Mitch's shows were like a guided tour of his brain, where he'd walk around and point out ridiculous things our brains have actually known all along, about things like foosball: "a combination of soccer and shish kabobs," and rotisserie chicken—"It's like a really morbid ferris wheel for chickens."

But to call Mitch a one-liner comic would be a disservice to the strong connection he made with his audience. Mitch liked the people in the audience. You could tell. This is rare for comedians. Mitch had long hair over his eyes and wore sunglasses and often spoke with his eyes closed. He occasionally referenced this on stage. "The reason I close my eyes sometimes onstage is that I have drawn a picture of an audience enjoying the show more on the back of my eyelids." To Mitch, his jokes were like his children. Some of them were accomplished. Some of them weren't. And some of them didn't even make a lot of sense. But he loved them all equally. He just loved jokes. When people didn't laugh, he'd pause a second and go, "All right . . . that joke was ridiculous."

Sometimes people would misunderstand Mitch. They'd ask, "What is he doing? Why is he lying on the floor? Why is he walking behind the curtain?" During one famous theater performance, the promoter placed a dozen seats on the stage, behind the performer—something about making more money by adding more front row seats. Mitch walked on stage and performed his entire show to those twelve people, ignoring the hundreds of people laughing hysterically behind him. Mitch straddled the line of what people considered a show, and no two shows were the same. He was the Iggy Pop of comedy. He was a rock star.

When I moved to New York I was confronted with the reality that only one club out of forty would give me regular spots. I knew that I needed to take my act on the road, the way I had seen all those other working comics do when I worked the door at a comedy club in college.

If I could just become a "middle act," the guy who performs after the emcee and before the headliner, I could make enough money to live. I needed to "middle." That's the technical name for it. I've always found "middling" to be a little bit of an insulting term. It implies mediocrity by definition. It's like if someone said, "What slot are you on the show?" and you're like, "I'm doing some mediocre comedy before the headliner."

"Yeah? You're mediocreing? Sounds like you're not very good."

"Well, no. That's misleading. To be specific, I'm neither good nor bad. I used to just emcee. I really sucked then."

Anyway, I wanted to middle but I wasn't experienced enough so I hit the road and worked as an emcee for about a year. I'd do ten minutes at the top of the show, remind people to turn off their cell phones, and bring out the other acts. I drove my mom's Volvo station wagon all over America, making somewhere between zero and three hundred dollars a week. It's really hard to convince club managers to let you middle when they see you as an emcee, so after these emcee engagements I'd drive hundreds of miles to do "guest spots" at clubs for free. I thought it was the only way to convince club managers that I could middle. Sometimes people enjoy the middle act more than the headliner, but almost nobody remembers an emcee. I was a traveling salesman of comedy, and I needed to make a sale if this comedy career delusion was going to pan out.

I caught a break from Lisa, the booker at Joker's Comedy Club in Dayton, Ohio. I had driven all the way there to do guest spots for the Amazing Johnathan, and he didn't want any openers. I spent one night operating the lights and doing sound cues in the back, and I wasn't even good at it.

At the end of the week I walked into Lisa's office, and she

felt bad too. She said, "I'm going to give you a week to middle." She flipped through her calendar and stopped in April. "We need someone for Mitch Hedberg."

My life couldn't possibly get better.

On April 23, 2002, I opened for Mitch at Joker's Comedy Club in Dayton, Ohio. I know the exact date because I had written it in my calendar six months before and stared at it whenever I had a free moment on the subway or in the back of a car. I highlighted it in blue and put stars next to it.

I tried to conceal my awe for Mitch the first time I picked him and his wife, Lynn, up to go to the club. Sometimes that's part of the job of an opening act, to drive the headliner from the hotel to the club. Which is really degrading if you think about that occurring in any other art form: "The central pieces in tonight's exhibition are done by painter Gustav Bringow and the supporting pieces are done by Bill Wilson. They'll both be arriving momentarily. Bill is picking Gustav up at the Holiday Inn Express in his mom's station wagon as part of his contractual obligation."

When the club owner asked me to pick up Mitch, I was in shock. First, I couldn't believe Mitch Hedberg was going to ride in my mom's Volvo station wagon. And second, I couldn't believe Mitch Hedberg rode in cars at all. I had always kind of envisioned him riding in a spaceship or just kind of teleporting onto stage. But I was thrilled to have the chance to pick him up. Picking Mitch up would make it more likely that he'd speak to me.

When I picked up Mitch and Lynn in my mom's Volvo wagon, I was surprised at their appearance. Their hair was still wet. They were disheveled and not ready for the show. *They were just like real people.*

The first show went pretty well, and afterward I asked Mitch and Lynn if they wanted to go bowling. I had just bought my own bowling shoes at a flea market so it seemed like a good opportunity. So we went, but I was so rattled to be bowling with my hero that I was awful. I rolled all kinds of ones and threes. I was so embarrassed. When we were walking out, Mitch said to me, "When you said you wanted to go bowling, I thought that you would be good at bowling." I laughed. It was like he made a Mitch Hedberg joke just for me.

That night Mitch was onstage and in the middle of his set he said, "Oh no, I got to go to the bathroom. Can someone come onstage and tell a joke?" There was this long gaping silence, then he said, "I'm serious, you guys. I really gotta go." And it's still silent. People didn't know what to do.

Backstage I turned to Lynn and said, "Are you gonna go up?"

"Will you?" she said.

"Okay."

I walked onstage and approached Mitch. He didn't know I was there because his eyes were closed. I said, "Mitch, I'm here."

He said, "Oh, thanks, man." And walked off like this was an everyday thing. The audience looked at me and I looked at the audience and everyone was laughing hysterically.

I took the microphone off the stand, looked down at the floor, and did my best Mitch Hedberg. "I am pretty good at tennis, but I will never be as good as the wall. The wall is relentless . . . There was a jar of jelly beans at the state fair that said 'Guess how many and you win the jar,' I was like, 'C'mon man, lemme just *have some.*'"

Like a lot of his fans, I knew Mitch's act so well that I could recite it on cue. It was thrilling. For one moment I was in Mitch's shoes. Mitch came back onstage, laughed, and said, "Aw, man. He did my best jokes."

A couple of years later, Mitch offered to perform at my CD release party at the Comic Strip in New York City. He flew himself in, put himself up at a hotel, and, when I tried to pay him, refused the money.

That night I opened up to Mitch and told him that my sleepwalking had gotten much worse and had started to become dangerous. There was clearly something going on that I wasn't dealing with. Mitch seemed to understand. It was as if, before that, Mitch didn't think that anything in my life could resemble anything in his life, but at that moment he did.

People always talked about Mitch's drug habit, but I never witnessed it, so I thought maybe it didn't exist, the way a kid puts his hands over his eyes and pretends no one's there. Mitch told me that he wanted to go on tour with me that fall. I couldn't believe it. I was blue highlighting it in my brain already. That night we talked about how we should play tennis together. We had planned stuff like this before, but except for our one bowling adventure, he had always cancelled.

I had this idea that if we went out on tour, we could play tennis, maybe see local sites, and somehow my non-drug-using habits would catch on. Even thinking about that now, it's delusional. It never would have happened. Mitch didn't want to stop. And no one was going to stop him, certainly not me.

• • •

I'm at the Friar's Club in Los Angeles. I've never been here before, but there's a memorial service being held for Mitch. I don't know if Mitch was a "friend" as much as he was someone I looked up to. Someone who sometimes called me back when I called him. Someone who took me under his wing in a slightly removed kind of way. To call him a friend would be a compliment to me, and I don't want to be presumptuous. Especially since he's dead. If he were here, I could imagine him saying, "I'm having a memorial service and Birbiglia is speaking. That is ridiculous," and then laughing, but in a mysterious way so I don't know if he's laughing with me or at me.

I'm up late every night combing the Internet for articles about Mitch. There are thousands of blog entries and message board postings, an outpouring of support from devastated fans who were touched by his work. I come across comedian Doug Stanhope's blog entry about Mitch's death.

Doug wrote: "Nobody has asked me how Mitch lived. And Mitch lived like a motherfucker. More than most any of us will live. That isn't sad or tragic."

Mitch was the number one search on Google that week. I learned that Mitch, who died at age thirty-seven, had heart problems from childhood that manifested in a deadly way when he combined heroin and cocaine in a hotel room in New Jersey. I didn't know this about Mitch. I didn't know anything. Mitch didn't talk about himself much and I was afraid to ask.

There was a second memorial service a few weeks later. The way Mitch's death was dragged out was testament to how much people loved him, but also to the fact that people didn't know quite what to do. Maybe if we kept having memorials, we'd get it right? I'm standing out front before the second service and Dave Attell says to me, "Are you gonna say something?"

I say, "I don't know. I feel like I didn't know him well enough."

Dave says, "Me neither, man."

It becomes clear to me in that moment that Dave looked up to Mitch as much as I did. He's feeling the same inadequacy I am. That he wasn't close enough to Mitch do him justice. That somehow there must be someone who understood Mitch more as a peer who could eulogize him the way he deserves.

But Dave speaks at the service. And so do I. We do our best, but it doesn't feel like enough.

When I think about the people I've looked up to in my life, they all tend to be people who can't stop. Mitch spent his final months playing comedy clubs, often doing two or three shows a night—three or four hours on stage. Not much rest, then on to the next city—not returning home for months at a time. Lynn once told me that Mitch never turned down a job. That he had been told "no" so often early in his career that he felt like if he didn't say "yes," he might not be given the opportunity to perform again.

It felt a lot like my life at that moment.

Some people are sad about Mitch's death. Some people are angry. Some people feel like he died the way he wanted to. But one thing is clear: we all looked up to Mitch, but maybe we should have looked straight at him.

SOMETHING IN MY BLADDER

When I was nineteen, my doctor found a malignant tumor in my bladder. But it's funny—stay with me—because I was a hypochondriac, and the funniest thing that can happen to you as a hypochondriac is that you get cancer, because it confirms every fear you've ever had and allows you to say to your family, "See? I told you! Remember last week when I was overtired and I thought I had rickets? I was probably right about that too. There are gonna be a lot of changes around here!"

I'm not a hypochondriac anymore. I avoid going to the doctor at all costs. I really think my willingness to visit the doctor was just based on positive associations with doctors as a kid. When you're a kid, going to the doctor is fun. My mother used to take me to Dr. Barrett's office and the waiting room would be packed. There were toys and blocks and lollipops. Dr. Barrett was funny. He'd look in my ear and say, "I see a kitty in there." *Wait, does he? Oh no, it's just a joke. This place is awesome.* My parents liked him because he went on his instincts. "He smelled sickness," my mom told me.

When I was three years old I came down with a gastro-intestinal virus. It came on all of a sudden. My family was all in the TV room in our house and I kept getting up to go to the bathroom. I had been potty-trained days before, so at first they thought maybe I was just showing off. At a certain point, Gina pointed out that I was having diarrhea. Minutes later I was throwing up repeatedly. And then my body went limp and I passed out on the rug. When they got me to the emergency room, Gina couldn't even get me to stand up on the scale. I was nearly unconscious. My parents were answering questions from the young fresh-faced interns: "Height? Weight? Allergies? Has he eaten anything today?" The question that set my dad off was "Was he breast-fed?"

"What does that have to do with anything? He is dehydrated! Get him an IV and get him in a room and get him a doctor!" My mother likes to point out that "those interns weren't using their instincts. They were just going by procedure, and sometimes that can be dangerous." They got me a doctor, a room, and an IV, and in a few hours I was pretty close to my usual self.

I remember from this point on very well, because there was a steady stream of visits, gifts, and attention. Gina read to me. My dad bought me a Curious George doll, which I kept for many years. I got balloons and pizza. Dr. Barrett came by and checked out the wildlife hiding in my ear. I stayed overnight and had a great time. It felt like a sleepover.

The next day I was good as new. Everyone else knew that I had a brush with death, but as far as I was concerned, I was having a pretty good week.

In 1998 I was driving home from college to see my parents for Christmas break when I stopped at a rest area and saw blood in my pee. I knew this could mean about five things and three of them meant I would die and the other two weren't exactly a trip to the Bahamas.

It was particularly disappointing because sometimes when I'm on road trips alone I'll have water-drinking contests with myself to see how clear I can make my pee. So I'll drink all this water and go to the urinal and my pee will be clear and I'll be like, *Bingo!* So when it was red, I thought, *Oh man. I lost big-time.*

I got very anxious. And when I get anxious I sometimes get this shallow breathing thing where I feel like I can't breathe and then I feel like I'm going to die because breathing is one of the building blocks of living.

I pulled into the driveway about 1:00 a.m. and my dad was sitting up reading. He's a bit of an insomniac. And I told him what happened. And he got a very grave look on his face because he's a doctor, so he knows about the Bahamas.

In the morning he took me to see his urologist friend, Dr. Del Vecchio. At the time I didn't know what urologists do. I'm older now, so some of my friends have gone for prostate exams, but when I was nineteen I was very naïve. In the examination room the nurse had me undress and put on a gown and I sat on that hygienic disposable paper. On the wall of the examination room there was a giant diagram of a penis, with all the parts labeled, and on the counter was a plastic model of a penis that clearly came apart like some sort of sexy science toy puzzle. They really cut to the chase in the urologist's examination room, and I tried to laugh. If this office were a movie, it would have been rated R.

After I spent a few minutes staring at penises Dr. Del Vecchio rushed in. He made some obligatory jokes about how bad my dad's putting was, and then he said, "Okay, Mike, I want you to put your hands on the table." I thought, *You're darn right I can put my hands on a table! This is totally no big deal. I wonder why he wants me to put my hands on the table?* And then he stuck his finger into the place where they do the prostate exams. And I didn't see that coming at all. No amount of staring at penis diagrams could have prepared me for that experience. So I shouted, *"Oh my God!"* And then he said, "Cut the theatrics!" And I felt so bad. I was like, "Sorry about the theatrics." As though I had intended it. Like, *This'll be my big moment. When he sticks his finger up my ass, I'll prove I should be the star of* Our Town*!*

I don't know how one is supposed to react in that situation. I mean, even if I were a robot, I'd be like, *"Sys-tem er-ror . . . oh-my-God."*

So the doctor said, "Listen, Mike, you gotta come in tomorrow morning for what's called a cystoscopy." And doctors always dress this stuff up. He said, "It's no big deal. You come in. They put an IV in. You fall asleep. You wake up. You eat a muffin. You go home." And I said, "Okay. I'm still a little shaken up by the table incident. But what's a cystoscopy?"

Then Dr. Del Vecchio picked up a rod about four feet long and said, "This has a camera on the end of it and we stick it through your urethra to look at your bladder." I thought, *urethra, urethra, I know I've heard of that part.* I glanced quickly to the wall of the giant diagram of the male anatomy and I was reminded that the urethra is a miniscule tube through which I had always peed. It did not seem to have adequate room to house camera equipment or a four-foot rod. And I just nodded and I thought, "*I feel like you glossed over a few details in the initial description. I feel like there was too much emphasis on the muffin and not enough mention of the fishing rod you're sticking into my number three body part on E's 'Top One Hundred Sexiest Body Parts.'*"

So I woke up the next morning and I felt like I couldn't breathe and my mom drove me to the hospital and the nurse put in the IV. For a while she couldn't find a vein, and that's always fun. It's just a stranger poking you with a needle and you just have to take it.

You're like, "Ow!"

Okay.

"Ow!"

Okay.

Eventually she found a vein. Apparently I have *one*.

While I was under, they found something in my bladder. You know, an item. So they decided to put me under deeper so that they could take it out. So they put me on the hospital equivalent of horse tranqs. When I woke up in the recovery room, I was sky-high with my mom—which was not the first time in my life I'd been high with my mom. But it was the first time she knew. I don't handle drugs very well. If you've ever been in a group of people smoking pot, I'm the guy who says, "Do you guys hate me? Why does my heart hurt? Is that rickets?" I'm not proud of it. It's just what I am. So I woke up in the recovery room but in my mind I was in a dance club. I shouted, "This place is awesome! We should come here all the time! Dad's always here!"

And my mom was like, "Shhh!" And I was like, "Do you hate me?"

So after I came down from the drugs, they discharged me from the hospital. And I still didn't know what had happened, and on the car ride home my mother said, "The doctor found something in your bladder." Whenever they tell you that, it's never anything good, like, "We found something in your bladder . . . and it's season tickets to the Yankees!"

Talk about highs and lows. I was literally the highest I've ever been in my life and then I was told I might die. Which is like being handed a pizza and then being shot in the face. So I started crying, and because I was crying, my mother started crying, because crying is like throwing up. It's a chain reaction.

For a week I had to wait for the results of the biopsy of the item they had found in my bladder. So for a week in my life I thought I might die—which is an incredible experience, if you ever have the chance to try it. You'll start talking to God even if you're not sure there's a God. You'll talk to anyone who might have more power than you, because you really want to cover your bases. You're like, *God? Allah? The elephant thing from Hinduism? L. Ron Hubbard? Harry Potter?* I'm brand-loyal to Jesus, but I'm not stubborn. If someone has a plan, I'll hear 'em out.

A week later, the biopsy came back. I was fortunate because while it was a malignant tumor, they had caught it early enough. I wouldn't have to take any further action except that every six months as a precaution I'd have to come in for a cystoscopy. The only difference was that, during the procedure, I would have to be awake. But it was okay because afterward, I could eat a muffin. So I did that . . . for a while.

. . .

SOMETHING IN MY BLADDER

In 2003 I started to get concerned about my sleep. I wasn't falling asleep until three or four in the morning, and I was waking up around six or seven. On top of all this, I started having these episodes where I would get out of my bed. There wasn't a lot of rest going on. I remember thinking, *Maybe I should see a doctor.* And then I thought, *Maybe I'll eat dinner.* And I went with dinner. For years.

THE PROMISE OF SLEEP

So I was having trouble sleeping and occasionally even getting out of my bed in my sleep. And I thought about seeing a doctor. And I didn't, but I did buy a book. It was called *The Promise of Sleep*.

I tried to read the book, but I ran into a little snag: I'm not great at reading. I have a small case of ADD. I have trouble focusing and my brain tends to wander. I remember when I was a kid, we'd read books in school:

There was Flopsy, Mopsy, Cottontail and Peter . . .

I'd have to stop right there. All I could think was, *If you're gonna name your rabbit Flopsy, are you really gonna name the second one Mopsy? Do you want everyone to hate them? And Peter is the only one who made it out okay in the naming process. Peter's like an investment banker now with a vacation home in the Hamptons. He's like, "I don't know those other rabbits!" And everyone asks him, "Aren't you Peter Rabbit?" and he's like, "No, no, no. I'm Peter McHuman." But really he is Peter Rabbit and he's just tucking his ears into a baseball cap.*

Anyway, while I was thinking about all that, the other kids READ THE BOOK.

I never got very good at reading, because when I would

voice my deficiency to my dad, he'd say, "Hush!" and I thought, *Okay, got it. Hush. I'm sure this problem will work itself out.*

Twenty years later, I picked up a much longer book called *The Promise of Sleep. Well, that's a very elusive title,* I thought. I mean, it *is* a promise, so that's good. But then again, the book isn't actually promising sleep. It's just putting it out there: *the* promise. Like, here's the promise that one could make. *I'm* not making it, but by all means feel free to make it to yourself, to your friends or whatever. If this book was sold in the cartoon world, you'd open it up and there'd be a big wooden mallet on a spring that would conk you on the head and you'd see little birds chirping around your head while you passed out. In some ways *The Promise* is more alluring than the famous self-help book *The Secret,* because the Secret could be anything. You could open that book up and it says, "The secret is you're a loser." *I'm a loser? I spent twenty-seven dollars on that?* By now you may be wondering, *is* that the Secret? How does Mike know so much about the Secret? Did someone tell him the Secret? Don't worry. They didn't. I *promise.*

The Promise of Sleep was written by a guy named Dr. Dement, which is a very unfortunate name for a man trying to instill calm in his readers. I think he could have opted for a pseudonym like Dr. Happy Sleep or Dr. Chamomile Tea. *I'm Dr. Chamomile Tea and I promise you'll sleep!* Thanks, Dr. C. Tea. I already have a nickname for you. My name is Mike but you can call me Tinkles.

Dr. Dement has four basic tips for healthier sleep. A few hours before bed, he says, turn off your phone, turn off the news, don't surf the Internet, and don't eat big meals—which just so happen to be my four favorite activities before I go to bed. You might even say that I'm addicted to these activities.

I check my phone messages and email about forty-five times a day. I don't even know what I'm expecting to get in these messages. Maybe Visa will call and say, "We just realized that we owe *you* money!" or I'll get an email from a high school classmate that says, "We've reconsidered and we've decided you were cool after all."

Whatever the case, I'm completely addicted to my phone. And I'm not the only one. I was at a movie recently and the guy next to me answered his phone in the middle of the movie and he answered it by saying, and I quote, he said, "Who dis?" Which means not only was he willing to talk to someone during the movie, he was willing to talk to *anyone* during the movie. I'm not sure what the past tense of *dis* is, but he did not care who it dus.

I actually bought a new phone recently. And my brother Joe wanted me to upgrade to the iPhone.

He was like, "You gotta get the iPhone."

"Why?"

"It's, you know, it's the fourth generation. It's got two cameras. You gotta get it."

"I still don't understand the reason."

"Don't you take pictures?"

"I thought you were talking about a phone."

(Pause) "It's both. You gotta get it."

I didn't get it. And don't get me wrong: I love cameras

and I love phones, but I also love pizza and ice cream and I've never seen them smashed together into one superfood.

When you go to buy anything these days, the guy's always like, "You know, it's *also* a camera." And it's a slippery slope. Like one day I'll go to the store to buy something and they'll be like, "It's also a camera."

"I just wanted a grapefruit."

"It's a camera-grapefruit. You take pictures of yourself eating the grapefruit, then you poop the pictures."

"That is the opposite of what I wanted."

I'm a purist when it comes to phones. I'm a *serious* phone talker. I don't need these distractions. Like crappy cameras and a calendar of events. The iPhone intimidates me because it *forces* you to multitask. And I'm not good at single-tasking. I can't walk and hold a drink at the same time. Is there an app for that? Some kind of cup holder that pulls out and stabilizes based on how awkward a conversation is? It senses I'm about to expound on my personal theory of bisexuality and it vibrates out of control. I'd buy that app.

I asked the guy at the store for the simplest phone they had. I said, "Can I have just the 'phone' phone?"

And he was so confused. He was like, "Um . . . This one is a dot-matrix printer."

I was like, "No . . . just the 'phone' phone."

He was like, "This one makes Jolly Rancher Minis."

I said, "No, just the 'phone' phone."

I ended up getting the simplest phone they have. But it still does nine things I don't understand. Nine. Maybe I'm a control freak, but that makes me nervous. I get worried: What if there's something in the phone I don't know about? What if there are bullets in the phone? Just hypothetically, what if I'm dialing a number and some passerby on the street is like, "You shot me!"

And I'm like, "Oh man, I was on the wrong screen. I thought that was a to-do list. I didn't know it was actual bullets."

And then he's like, "You gotta get a doctor!"

And I'm like, "Good idea, where is that—under Tools?"

Phones have gotten way too complicated. They've got all these ringtones to choose from and I'm not really a ringtone guy. I'm purely a vibrations man. I don't even understand why people have rings on their phones. We don't need an electronic version of the *Miami Vice* soundtrack poisoning the peaceful silence we're all enjoying. A vibration is loud enough if you think about it. It's not as if a vibration is soundless. By definition vibration *is* sound. Besides, it feels nice when it vibrates, kind of a mini-massage, a little tingle to remind you you're alive.

I love that little vibration. I'm addicted to that vibration. My phone vibrating in my pocket feels like being woken up as a kid on Christmas morning. *Wake up, Mike, you've got a telephone call! It could be anyone.*

Growing up, cable television was a luxury that only a few people we knew could afford. Not us—our family had the giant rotating antenna mounted on our garage, with that spinning dial which would make it turn to pick up the best signal. When our TV wasn't working, my sisters would just send Joe behind the set with a butter knife for a screwdriver, some electrical tape, and some simple instructions, "Make it work." Joe became the best seven-year-old TV repairman in Shrewsbury.

My neighbor Leslie had cable. It was fantastic. Our favorite show was *You Can't Do That on Television,* but it seemed to me you could do anything on cable television. You could be flipping through the seemingly endless channels and at any moment you might hear the s-word or stumble across some exposed breasts. Whatever this new television service cost, it was worth it.

I asked my mom if we could get it and she said, "Like fun are we getting cable. That stuff is junk." She talked about cable TV like it was porn. I think she was right.

I have cable TV in my apartment now and it's sucking my life away. Because it makes me think things that are unimportant are *really important.* I'm like, *I have to know about the sexiest music videos from the eighties.* What would happen if I didn't know about the sexiest music videos from the eighties? Would that mean I'm not sexy? E! answers questions that you were never going to ask, like, "I wonder how the show *Full House* was made?" Oh, in a studio with sets designed to look like the inside of a house? Fascinating!

What's perhaps more scary is cable news, because, while dealing in minutiae just as meaningless, they claim to be important. One trick is they use these flashy graphics and laser sound effects like *"Pachoo!"* or *"Brrrr-Bing!"* And they treat every story with the same level of importance. They'll be like, *"Pachoo!* Are your kids having sex at the mall?" I don't even have kids, but I'm like, *Are they? I gotta make sure they're not having sex at the mall. Like fun are they having sex at the mall!* And then the next story will be like, *"Pachoo!* Terrorists blow up bus." And I'm like, *Wow, that really puts the mall sex in perspective. That is much worse.*

Cable news has another trusty trick, which is that they hook you in with questions you couldn't possibly know the answers to. They'll be like, "*Pachoo!* Do you know what's in your soup?"

I'm like, *Oh my God. I guess I don't know what's in my soup. I gotta stick around. I thought maybe broth but I wasn't 100 percent . . . What is this, a commercial for Toyota? Okay, I'll watch this, just as long as you tell me what's in my soup.*

And then they'll be like, "*Pachoo!* It's broth."

I'm like, *I knew it!* I knew it was broth, but I wasn't 100 percent. I'm glad I stuck it out.

And then they'll be like, "*Pachoo!* Do you know what's in your broth?"

I can't believe this! How long do I have to watch to find out all the answers? But they never tell you the answers because they know if you knew the answers you'd change the channel or turn off the television. But I don't turn off the television.

I watch it at airports, in hotels, in my apartment. I can't do a four-minute treadmill run without checking in on Headline News, which is really the perfect network for the micro workout. You flip it on and the guys says, "Earth still spinning, wars still going on, planet still headed toward total death and destruction. Those are your headlines!" But at a certain point I realized that I needed more than this. I needed to do something at the same time. Which is why I started spending more time on the Internet.

The Internet, much like cable TV, is an infinite well of nothingness. And when you're there, you're convinced that it's something. It's like getting drunk. You're like, *I'm gonna go over here. And over there . . . and over here!* And after four hours, you're like, *I don't even know what happened. I gotta clear my history.*

I always have these grand ambitions for the next time I'm going to be online. Like, *The next time I'm on the Internet, I'm going to look up healthy recipes and gyms in my neighborhood.* And then I go online and I'm like, *I'm gonna Google myself again.* And I don't even Google myself anymore. I'm at the next level. I get Google alerts. Last year someone wrote on their blog that they had come to my show and that they enjoyed it, but that I was "pudgy and awkward." I got that as a Google alert.

It was like, "*Pachoo!* You're p'awkward!"

Thanks for the heads-up, Google. Not feeling great about myself to begin with, but perhaps I did need a reminder.

Well, with a laptop on my crotch and the news pumped up to a volume level of thirty-four, I can effectively take in a huge amount of nothing. I can multitask nothingness to an extent that the writers of *The Matrix* wouldn't even understand. And while that's all going on, I can grab my phone in case I need some pizza.

The last item on Dr. Dement's list of things to avoid before bed is big meals. This is especially tough for me.

Whenever I tell people I'm trying to lose weight, they say, "You don't need to lose weight . . . that much." And it's true, I don't have a weight problem, but I am the guy who could really put the brakes on an orgy. Everyone would be like, "Was he invited? Why is he eating a stuffed crust pizza? That is not sexy at all."

I come from a family of bingers. The Birbiglia family is Italian, but we're not real Italian, we're Olive Garden Italian. We don't eat capellini primavera. We eat unlimited salad and breadsticks and drink a mean white zinfandel.

When I was in high school, my father took our family on a trip to Italy. My brother Joe was spending a semester in Florence and my dad thought it would be the perfect opportunity to visit the motherland. Our whole lives, my dad had espoused the virtues of Italy. How Italians treat each other. How cultured Italians are. And most of all, how they eat. We've been regulars at the Olive Garden since its proliferation in the early nineties. And when we go, my dad attempts to order food with an authentic accent. He'll be like, "I'll have the *pasta fa-jool.*" I'm like, "We're sitting in a strip mall in Hyannis, Massachusetts, between a Build-A-Bear and a Spencer Gifts. You'll have the pasta fag-eee-oh-lee like everybody else." So there we were, the Birbiglia family, educated at the Olive Garden, and now we were ready to go to the source. Joe made arrangements for us to eat at one of the finest restaurants in Florence. We looked at the menu put together by a world-class chef, a menu thoughtfully designed for hours and time-tested through years of serving discerning customers, and my dad looked at the waiter who didn't speak English and said, "I'd like a spaghetti with tomato sauce and one meatball and one sausage." Joe jumped in and explained to my dad that the waiter didn't speak English and that it would be better to choose something on the menu since we didn't want to offend the artistry of the chef.

My dad looked at Joe sternly and said, "Tell him *one*"—my dad slowed down as though now Joe no longer spoke English either—*"meatball . . . and one sausage."* We had traveled four thousand miles and he was ordering his Olive Garden favorite. Joe spoke to the waiter in Italian and, without offending, cobbled together some combination of two dishes that we shoveled onto one plate. I didn't blame my dad. He's like me. He doesn't like interesting food. He likes comfort food. And he likes it now.

Pizza is probably my biggest weakness. I *love* pizza. I would marry pizza, but it would just be an elaborate ploy to eat her whole family at the reception. What's not to love about pizza? I mean, look at the ingredients: you got cheese, which is comfy and salty. It's more or less superfatty concentrated milk. Then you have crust, which is bread. Bread is always a winner in my book. I once went to Thanksgiving dinner at the house of our family friends the Naples and ate only dinner rolls. I'm not exaggerating; it was the best Thanksgiving ever.

So basically you've got cheese curds piled on dinner rolls with some tomato-flavored custard mixed in and it tastes *amazing*.

When I'm traveling, I will almost always order a pizza at the hotel or motel I'm staying at. As a matter of fact, my favorite time to eat pizza is *the moment before I fall asleep*. I think that could be a menu item: "pizza until you fall asleep." And you call and order it and leave the door unlocked and you time it so the delivery guy walks in with a pizza shaped like a travel pillow and you wrap it around your neck and you eat it while doing neck rolls until you fall asleep.

Sometimes when people find out how much I love pizza, they'll give me a wink and a nod, maybe pull me aside and say something like, "I understand. I'm a foodie too." A *foodie*, if you've never heard the term, is a trendy word for a gourmet or a food connoisseur. But I'm not a foodie. I wish I were. Being a foodie implies that I have good taste in food, which I don't. Foodies are interesting and open to trying various dishes to diversify their palate. That's not me. I want to eat the same thing until I pass out.

I'm a binger. I love the act of eating. I love world-class pizza and I also love pizza from a gas station, provided the warming bulb is working. I will eat anywhere.

I particularly like chain restaurants. They completely understand mass consumption and have amazing offers for people like me. For starters, bottomless soda. I just like the word *bottomless*. I like the implication that maybe this meal will never end. And combining it with *soda,* which is a nutritionless but flavorful beverage, makes for a sexy phrase for bingers like me.

Get me some bottomless nothingness! And make it fast. I'm living over here!

When it comes to eating I have no self-control. I simply can't drive by a Cheesecake Factory without stopping. I love their chicken sandwich the size of a soccer ball and their piece of cake as large as an entire cake. I love the Factory's generous portions. They're like, "We *could* sell grilled cheese sandwiches for a buck fifty, *or* we could stuff a loaf of bread with three pounds of mozzarella and call it the Mozza Mountain." And hey, if the Factory says it's one serving, who am I to question them? They're making this stuff to factory specifications.

Sometimes I'll go somewhere exotic like P. F. Chang's, the pan-Asian staple of Chainville city, USA. Though I won't use the chopsticks. I don't like chopsticks because I can't get food down my throat fast enough. It's almost like those pan-Asians don't get it.

I've spoken to a lot of dieticians over the years, and most of them will say, "You can eat hamburgers. You can eat pizza. You can eat fried chicken. The key is that you don't *binge*." And I'm thinking, *That's my move. Bingeing is the best play I have in my book.*

Even now as I type this, I'm sitting at a chain called Starbucks, a quaint local coffee shop that does a decent blueberry muffin. Actually, the thought of food makes me want to get up and order some food, even though I ate lunch an hour ago and the Starbucks offerings today don't look particularly fresh. I'm considering the cinnamon swirl muffin or the banana bread. But I'll probably go with something healthier. The fruit and cheese plate. I will devour the cheese and crackers and then slowly insert pieces of fruit into my mouth as punishment.

They say bingeing stems from the self-perpetuating idea that eating a lot of food might fix something or fill some void that needs filling. I'm not sure what void they're talking about, but man, does that make me hungry.

I actually still have *The Promise of Sleep* in my backpack. It's beat-up and weatherworn. I still haven't *finished* it, though I have skipped around a bunch. Maybe while I was obsessing over my addictions to vibrating phones and mind-numbing cable news and sleep-pillow-shaped pizza, the other kids with sleep disorders . . . read the book.

SLEEPWALK WITH ME

I'm going to tell you this one last story. This one is particularly personal. It's actually the most terrifying thing that ever happened to me. It's one of those very rare moments in your life where in retrospect you're like, *"What the hell?"* But at the time you think, *I guess I'll continue living.* It's like if you went to the dentist and he asked you to take your pants off and you say to yourself, *Um . . . He's got a degree . . . But I'm gonna make a note of this, because this seems crazy.*

It's probably the first event in my life where I fully understood my father's warning: *Don't tell anyone.*

It's January 20, 2005, and I'm in Walla Walla, Washington—which is a place. I'm staying at a hotel called La Quinta Inn, and some people correct me when I say that. They say, "No, no, it's not *La Kwin-ta,* it's *La Keen-Tah*" and *that's not fair. You can't force me to speak Spanish. I didn't press two.* So I'm at *La Keen-tah Een* in *Wy-a Wy-a Wash-eeen-tahn.* It's one a.m. and I'm lying in bed. I have just performed at five colleges in four days and I'm exhausted. But I'm not going to sleep because I'm an insomniac. I'm sitting up in my bed with my laptop warming my thighs. I'm Googling myself. I'm watching the news. And I'm eating a pizza. At the same time.

And I fall asleep.

I have a dream that there is a guided missile headed toward my room and there are all these military personnel in the room. I jump out of bed and say, "What's the plan?"

And the general in charge turns to me and says, "The missile coordinates are set specifically on you."

This wasn't the first time I had walked in my sleep.

Let me start at the beginning. It all started around the time I met Abbie.

When I was in college I fell in love with Abbie.

Falling in love for the first time is a completely transcendent experience. It's like eating pizza-flavored ice cream. Your brain can't even process that level of joy. Love makes people do crazy things like kill other people or shop at Crate & Barrel. I think on some level it makes us all delusional. Deep down, our whole lives, no matter how low our self-esteem gets, we think, *I have a secret special skill that no one knows about and if they knew they'd be amazed.* And then eventually we meet someone who says, "You have a secret special skill."

And you're like, "I know! So do you!"

And they're like, "I know!"

And then you're like, "We should eat pizza ice cream together." And that's what love is. It's this giant mound of pizza-flavored ice cream and delusion.

I fell for Abbie immediately because she had this big, beautiful smile. It seemed like her teeth were bigger than her head, but in a really sexy way.

Abbie and I were both in theater at school. My first month at Georgetown I saw signs for auditions for an improv comedy troupe and thought, *Well, of course I should be in that.* I auditioned, not really knowing what I was doing. In high school I had been in *Our Town* because they were short on people and needed someone to play Howie Newsome, the milkman. I had taken drama because I heard it was easy. And it was. Plays are much easier to read than books. There are only five to ten words a line and they're triple-spaced. I'd read plays like cereal boxes. I thought, Oedipus Rex *is fantastic! I don't know what the hell it's about, but it's fast! Bring it on,* Angels in America*! Glengarry Glen-*so-few-pages*!* The acting part was fun too because I could basically just mess around. In life when I acted like a loud idiot I got in trouble. In drama they gave me course credit.

When I got to college I discovered a more serious group of actors. So serious, they were . . . gay. It always makes me laugh when people are surprised that their favorite Hollywood stars are gay. I'm quick to point out, "Remember how sixty-five percent of the drama club in high school was gay? Well, they graduated." Anyway, I made it into this improv group and that's how I met Abbie. My fellow improvisers and I hosted this big event on campus called the Washington DC A Cappella Fest, where a cappella groups from schools across the country would blow audiences away in the seven hundred-seat Gaston Hall and then bore people to death at the a cappella parties for five hours afterward with their "deeper cuts." Abbie and her friend Hannah saw me playing a basketball player in a sketch and the sight gag must have done something for Abbie because the next day she recognized me in a coffee shop and said, "Hello."

Since people rarely wanted to talk to me, I quickly tried to come up with some artsy conversation.

"Have you guys seen this play *Harvey*? It's great."

Abbie said, "I'm the star of it."

I stumbled, "Well . . . then you've seen it a lot."

They laughed, thinking I had planned the joke, but I really didn't recognize Abbie from the play. She had played Veta Louise Simmons and her performance was so transformative that it was nothing like she was offstage. Onstage she was a meticulous know-it-all and offstage she was a cool, adorable girl who seemed to want to know me. A little.

So I fell for Abbie immediately. And I kept running into her on campus because I was following her. I would say, "Hey! We should hang out sometime like not by mistake" and she would say no, which was hot, because then I knew she was sensible.

But I wore her down. Well, I tricked her.

She had said no so many times that I threw an off-speed pitch. I said, "Hey, we should go to church sometime." I hadn't been to church much since I was a kid, but Georgetown had a really nice chapel on campus. "That way if the date doesn't go well, maybe we'll get something out of the homily?"

She laughed.

And we went to church on our first date.

She was pretty focused on the priest and I was pretty focused on her, and when the mass ended, it was raining. I had remembered to bring an umbrella, so I was able to walk her home in the rain. And as we walked home, she held on to my arm. It was the happiest I'd ever been.

Abbie lived off campus as she was a junior—I was a freshman—and when we got there, I didn't want the date to end, so I told her about a ballroom dance class I had taken earlier that day, and I started showing her some of the moves. We didn't kiss, but we did the cha-cha without music in her well-lit living room, which is somehow even sexier than kissing.

I walked home in the rain and I had all this energy. So I went to the computer lab in my dorm and I wrote an email to Joe, saying, "I just went out with the girl I'm going to marry."

Abbie had to convince me to have sex for the first time. It was like a role reversal of the abusive boyfriend from the eighties high school movies where the girl says, "Devin, I can't." And Devin points out, "But you can." Except she was Devin. And I was Molly Ringwald. I was always afraid of sex in high school. I was one of those kids who didn't even understand the concept of sex. My nickname was "the math jockey." And what's sad about that is that I wasn't even good at math, which means I was not the sex jockey.

Abbie and I decided that for our first time we would go to a bed and breakfast, because nothing alleviates the fear of having sex for the first time like a really elaborate plan. We went to this place called the Philip Smith House. It was run by these two gay men named David and Leon. They had a really cute partnership where David cooked breakfast and Leon fucked David. At least it seemed that way.

We drove Abbie's mint-green Taurus to the Outer Banks of North Carolina. We sang along with the radio. We arrived at the B&B and took out their bicycle built for two. We did everything you do on a romantic weekend away.

Except have sex.

At all costs we were both committed to using a condom. I wanted to because I was afraid of getting my girlfriend pregnant. Abbie wanted to because she was *really* afraid of getting pregnant. So we brought plenty of condoms and got started with the business at hand. It wasn't a sexy turn of events. Somehow it felt like a medical operation where we were trying to insert parts of me into parts of her, and frankly it wasn't working because every time we would get something started, we would go to put on a condom and realize one of the reasons people don't use condoms is because they make you think about what you're doing. I find that once you think about it, sometimes your parts lose their excitement for the project. We tried and failed about three times and finally she said, "Who cares about this? Let's just go to the beach."

So we went to the beach, thinking it would be soothing. You know that thing they say about sex and pizza: when it's good it's good; when it's bad it's still good. Well, I thought that was also true of beaches. But I was wrong. We were sitting on the beach and we got attacked by bees. On a beach. I had just been emasculated entirely and now I'm running away from these half-inch insects. I have a new theory about sex: when it's good it's good; when it's bad, don't go to the beach, because there could be bees there.

One week later, when we got back to school, Abbie and I had sex for the first time the way everyone should have sex for the first time: we got drunk and forgot it ever happened.

It was clunky and awkward. But we were in love.

. . .

Abbie didn't believe in marriage. She was a Women's Studies minor and she believed that marriage was a social construct designed by a patriarchy that oppresses women. Thus, all ideas in this construct are null and void.

Abbie had a lot of theories like this. She would meet up with me after class and say things like "Starfishes are bisexual, and I think it's safe to say that people are bisexual too." And I would say, "I don't know much about starfishes, but when I see a naked dude, I don't get a boner."

These discussions were so long and drawn out that finally I enrolled in a Women's Studies class called Anthropological Perspectives on Gender. It was taught by a Professor Woods, who was very confused as to why I had enrolled in a class comprised entirely of women and two gay dudes. Little did she know that I was trying to build cunning arguments to use against my women's studies girlfriend using the enemy's own information.

We read books with titles like *Women and Poverty* and *Fraternity Gang Rape,* the kind of uplifting literature often overlooked by the Chicken Soup for the Soul series. I got pretty obsessed with it. I was like, "They're right! This *is* bullshit! The male patriarchy is keeping us down!"

I would read all the recent feminist articles and occasionally there'd be one in the school paper. I remember one time one of the standout students in this department wrote a really explicit article in the school paper about how she'd been harassed by some guys on campus and how the school had ignored it. It really affected me. I thought, *That girl is awesome. She's so brave. I should tell her.*

Occasionally I would see this brave writer around campus and I'd try to build up the confidence to tell her how much

I appreciated her piece in the paper. Then I'd get shy and wouldn't say anything. Late one night toward the end of the year I was walking home to my dorm and I saw her on a secluded path. I got up the nerve to say something. And there was no one around, and I knew it would be kind of awkward, but I thought, *She's graduating. I shouldn't hold in a compliment. This may be my only chance.*

I stopped her and said, "I know you don't know me, but that whole piece you wrote about you being harassed by all those guys, it really meant a lot to me, and—"

And she said, "That wasn't me."

And I said, "All right, cool. See you around."

The girl who actually wrote the article did graduate and I never told her how much I liked her piece. But the girl who I thought wrote it had a few more college years in her, and I would see her around every now and then. We had that special bond two people have when they've encountered one another once and one of them has told the other inaccurately that he admired her bravery in regards to being harassed by a group of men.

As a result of my association with Abbie I became a feminist activist. There was an event on campus called "Take Back the Date," which was this conservative group's response to "Take Back the Night," an internationally held march against rape and violence against women. "Take Back the Date" didn't have much of a leg to stand on, parodying a group whose only goal was to raise awareness about violence against women. Their unofficial position on date rape was, "It doesn't happen on *every* date!" Their platform was that we needed to end the era of "hooking up" and go back to the good old days of "dating." "Remember the good old days when women were subservient but sassy?" *Who knew this was an issue?* I didn't. No one was hooking up with me except Abbie. And those were dates, I think.

Anyway, Abbie hated this rival women's group. So Abbie and her friends decided to crash the Take Back the Date event. So I went along too. As we walked over to the student center for this event, we perused the Take Back the Date pamphlet and we started picking it apart. First in ways that made sense, but when we ran out of points that made sense, our criticisms became pretty irrational.

One of the women in our group looked at the pamphlet and said, "This is so stupid. Who are they to tell us how we should see each other romantically?"

Fair point.

Then someone said, "How come there are no gay relationships in the pamphlet? Can't gay people go on dates?"

Okay, less strong of a point. But okay.

Then someone was like, "How come there are no drawings of black people in the pamphlet? Can't black people date?"

This is where the wheels fell off the trailer. I don't think the Take Back the Daters were racist per se, but that didn't stop us. We were like, "Yeah! Why no black people?"

With this bit of momentum we walked into the event, taking seats like regular pro-daters and blending in with the crowd.

After the panel of pro-dates spoke, they took questions. This is always the activist's sweet spot. The Q&A!

First question.

Someone from our group stood up and said, "This is homophobic. It's offensive to women. And it's a step back for women everywhere!"

It wasn't so much a question as it was a statement. And with that, our entire group stood and started walking toward the exit. I hadn't been told we were going to leave. To make matters worse, while they were leaving, Abbie shouted to the stage, *"How come there are no black people on the cover?"* The pro-daters were confused. I was even more confused and, sadly, I was the only person left in our group still there, the lone representative of the anti-daters. I was like, "I'm with the people who hate dating. I'm actually dating one of the anti-daters. Okay . . . so, good luck with everything." I slunk out the back of the room and reconvened with my fellow protestors at a local bar.

Abbie and I argued about feminist issues a lot, and it was productive. It made me think that if people had more open talks about gender, we wouldn't have so many books about the various planets men and women are from. One time our discussion of gender issues got so contentious that I actually started crying. We were talking about marriage and she told me that she didn't believe in it and was never going to get married. I think the reason I was crying was that before I met her, I didn't believe in it either.

Abbie and I were living together and it was a secret. This was her idea. She said, "We should live together." Now, what I should have said was "I don't know if my parents would go for that because they're very conservative." What I did say was "Yeah!"

So when my parents visited, we'd put all her stuff in the bedroom and close the door to the bedroom. It worked. And it was exciting. But lying to my parents caused me anxiety. That was when I started walking in my sleep.

It was the fall of 1998. I was secretly living with Abbie, secretly working at a comedy club, and nearly failing out of school all at the same time. I started having this recurring dream that there was a hovering, insectlike jackal in my bedroom. Each time I had this dream, I would jump up on our bed and strike a karate pose. I had never taken karate, but I had the books from a book fair. So in this book-fair karate pose, I'd say, "Abbie! There's a jackal in the room!" She got so used to this that she could talk me down while remaining asleep.

"Michael, there's no jackal. Go to sleep," she'd mumble.

"Are you sure?" I'd ask, continuing to hold my karate pose.

"Yes, Michael, there's no jackal. Go to sleep."

And I would lie down, *knowing* there was a jackal hovering right above, ready to swoop down and kill us.

When I would have these episodes, Abbie would say, "Doesn't that sleepwalking stuff seem strange?"

"Yeah."

"Do you think maybe you should see a doctor about that?"

"Yeah, I will, but right now I'm really busy."

In addition to lying to our parents about living together, we also lied about our career plans. Abbie was pre-med but had decided that she wanted to be an actress. And I was an English major but wanted to be a comedian. So Abbie started applying to grad school for acting. I was working the ticket window at the DC Improv. I kept this a secret for a while one night I let my guard down and mentioned my side job to my dad casually on the phone. It didn't go so well. "Goddammit, Michael. School is your number one priority. Sounds like you need some *reality testing*!"

I said, "Okay," but it wasn't my number one priority.

I wanted a career in comedy, though I had no idea how to get there. Somehow, I figured, on the day of my college graduation they would hand me my diploma and I would hop in the back of a black van waiting for me outside the front gates of school and it would take me to New York.

There was one big problem: Abbie had been accepted in a graduate acting program in DC, which meant that while I escaped to New York, she would still be in school. I hadn't told Abbie about my plan. I mean, I had told other people when they asked and Abbie was there. But I never said it to her directly. And on graduation day the issue came to a head.

Abbie and I were at our apartment packing up the last few things of our still-secret living arrangement, and Abbie said, "So I guess I'll see you . . . ," and then she started bawling. This destroyed me. She was the girl who saw my secret special skill and I couldn't handle her crying.

I held on to her and said, "It's what I have to do right now."

She said through tears, "You didn't even tell me. You were just going to leave and not even tell me."

I said, "It's hard to talk about because I love you and I want to be with you."

"Then what are you going to do?"

"I don't know."

"We should just break up then."

And then she went cold. Coldness was worse than crying

because crying at least had a pulse. The patient was dying on the operating table and so I took out the electrical revival thingies and said, "We can make it work."

She said, "What do you mean?"

"Well, I can still work at the DC Improv half the time and commute to New York and live on Gina's couch."

This was pretty close to a lie.

There was almost no way I could make that work, with how difficult it would be to make my way in a new field and move between cities and make a living at the same time. But I said it. And she got less cold. She was coming back to life. So I embellished toward the warmth. I said, "I'll do anything to make it work."

We were alive. Two patients in critical condition on the operating table, telling ourselves, *We're doing fine. We're in love.*

Two years later Abbie graduated from school and moved in with me in New York. We lived in Brooklyn in this tiny one-bedroom and it was comfy. We had two cats and a big puffy couch. And we made our first major purchase. We bought a TiVo. We had gone through some rough patches in the past few years, but living together was going to fix everything.

One night I had this dream that I was in the Olympics, in some kind of arbitrary event like dustbustering. And they told me I got third place and I climbed up onto the third-place podium. Even in my dreams I don't win. In my wildest dreams I place. And then the Olympic judge approached me and said, "Actually you got second place."

I moved over to the second-place podium and it started wobbling. And wobbling. And I woke up as I was falling off the top of our bookcase in our living room, I landed on the top of our TiVo, which sat on our hardwood floor. It broke into pieces and I was totally disoriented. It was like one of those stories you hear where people black out drinking and they wake up in Iowa and they don't know where they are and they're looking around, thinking, *Oh no . . . Hardee's.* But it was in my living room. I thought, *Oh no . . . TiVo pieces.* And I went to bed.

Abbie woke me up in the morning and said, "Michael, what happened to the TiVo?" "I got second place," I said. "And I am really sorry."

This was the first time I thought, *This seems dangerous. Maybe I should see a doctor.* And then I thought, *Maybe I'll eat dinner.* And I went with dinner. Partly because of my fear of doctors based on the bladder incident I explained earlier. And partly because sleepwalking is a terrifying concept. Your body is making a decision that is distinctly different from your conscious mind's. Your conscious mind is like, *We're gonna rest for a while,* and your body's like, *We're going skiing!*

Sleepwalking also involves your brain, which is a very precarious area. The list of fun and easily fixed brain diseases is very short. So I didn't see a doctor. That's when I bought *The Promise of Sleep* by Dr. Dement, who, like I said earlier, told me to turn off the news, turn off the Internet, turn off my phone, and to not eat big meals—the tetrad of my favorite pre-sleep activities. There is a lot in *The Promise of Sleep* about anxiety and how anxiety can be a major heightening factor with sleep issues. At this point, I was experiencing the height of my anxiety.

I was twenty-three years old and it was becoming clear that Abbie wanted to get married. I could tell because there were two shows that kept popping up on our TiVo and one was called *A Wedding Story* and the other was called *A Baby Story.* These are reality shows on the TLC network about weddings and babies. And they're not the most exciting depictions of weddings. It's always two people whose names have some kind of alliteration. Like, Tommy and Tammy! And they'll ask Tommy, "Tommy, what's your favorite thing about Tammy?"

And Tommy will say, "I saw that Tammy was beautiful on the outside and now I know that she is also beautiful on the inside."

And they'll ask Tammy, "Tammy, what's your favorite thing about Tommy?"

And Tammy will say, "I didn't know what Prince Charming was until I met Tommy and now I know what Prince Charming is."

I've never seen *Baby Story,* but I imagine it's a bunch of babies saying, "I didn't know I was a baby until I was a baby and now I'm a baby."

I knew Abbie wanted to get married and I knew my *parents* wanted me to get married, which was strange because it never seemed like *they* wanted to be married to each other. I always thought they were going to split up when I was a kid because Vince would fly off the handle suddenly and no one knew why.

He'd shout something like, "Goddammit, I'm eatin' pretzels!" And I would think, *Is he angry? Is he hungry? What is the emotion being expressed?*

My whole life my dad was constantly searching for the portable phone. He'd yell, "Where's the goddamn portable phone?" My mother's role in the household was to find the portable phone, and when I was in high school someone invented that pager function that locates the phone and I thought they'd get divorced and on the divorce papers under "reason" he'd write, "I found the phone. Goddammit!"

But they never got divorced. They've been married forty years.

That is too long.

If the people who invented marriage knew that people would be married for forty years, they'd be like, "This isn't what we intended at all." Back then, people only lived to be forty, if they were lucky. Those marriage inventors would be so confused. They'd be like, "Forty years?! When were they married? As babies? We don't approve of babies marrying one another!"

Maybe I'm cynical but there's a part of me that thinks that in the future, marriage will be the new divorce. People will say things like, "Yeah, I'm pretty messed up. My parents are still together."

And you'll say, "Wow. That sounds really hard. Is it a first marriage?" And they'll say, "Yeah, it's rough. I have this fear that I'll love someone and then eventually hate them."

I'm comfortable saying that, by the way, because it's not just my family. I grew up in a very Catholic town where *everyone* was afraid to get divorced because it would reflect badly on their family. You know what else reflects badly on the family:

them yelling so loud I can hear it at the paint store three blocks away.

But my parents really wanted me to get married. I think my dad thought if I got married, maybe my wife could get me to wear a collared shirt. My mother had other motivations. At one point she actually offered a prize to whichever one of her children got married first. The prize was a blue baby bonnet, which may have revealed a little bit about her ulterior motives. She even set my sister Gina up on a date, and when she got home my mother said, "How did it go?"

Gina said, "Well, I don't think it's going to work out because at the end of the date he called me Christina."

And my mother said, "Well, you look like a Christina!"

My mother was willing to rename her daughter so that Gina-Christina could marry some random dude who didn't know her name.

I knew my father wanted me to get married. Not because he said it—he never would have been that explicit—but he'd say these kind of cryptic things. On one occasion my father and I were watching golf in my parents' living room, and he looked over at me and said, "Michael, at a certain point, you got to zig or zag." It came out of nowhere like a UFO.

"Wait, about what?" He just stared at me. The UFO was gone and all I knew was that I had to zig or zag. I didn't even know which was zigging or which was zagging but I knew it was important.

Abbie also wanted me to zig or zag. This was troubling because I had always wanted to marry Abbie from the moment we started seeing each other, but when the moment came nearer and fell into focus, I started to feel claustrophobic.

I started to develop this fear that maybe marriage would be like school.

I remember when I was real little and I thought, *Maybe someday I'll get to go to school.*

And then I went to school.

And the first week, I asked, "How much longer do I have to go to school?"

And they said, "Seventeen more years."

And I thought, *Oh no. I never should have gone to school.*

Now I found myself thinking, *Maybe I should break up with Abbie.*

Around this time I went to my brother Joe's wedding. If you're ever in a relationship that seems to be moving toward marriage and you're not comfortable moving in that direction, don't go to my brother Joe's wedding. Because it'll come up. Marriage was practically the theme of Joe's wedding. I remember we were taking family photos and my mother pulled me into a photo and said, "Michael, do you want Abbie in the photo?"

I said, "Yes," but not fast enough.

There was a slight pause.

And there was a reason for the pause.

That week I had just returned from a month on the road. I had driven Abbie's mint-green Taurus across the country from club to club, making just a little more than gas money and living in awful hotels. But I loved it.

And one night I was backstage at this club and this waitress came up to me to take my order and we were making small talk and she said, "I just got back from my other job, which is at Hooters, which is crazy because one of my boobs is bigger than the other. Isn't that crazy?"

I said, "Yeah."

She said, "Do you want to see them?"

Now, whenever anything so out of the ordinary occurs in my life, I'm always suspicious that it's a setup of some kind. Like this girl would take out her boobs and say, "What do you think, *math jockey*? Is one of the boobs *greater than* the other?"

I said to myself, *Mike, you are not going to give up your relationship with a girl who sees your secret special skill and can talk you down from a karate pose for a girl with one boob greater than the other.* So I said, "Actually I shouldn't be here, because I have a girlfriend."

"Don't worry," she said, "I know the drill."

Which blew my mind. Because I did not know the drill. I thought, *What is this drill and how can I find out more about this drill?*

But I stopped myself and I left the situation. A few hours later, after several drinks, I reentered the situation and ended up in the back of Abbie's Taurus with this girl. I was overcome with guilt and shame but I also felt like this kind of thing might happen again and I *knew* I shouldn't be getting married. But I couldn't say it.

So here I was at my brother's wedding and they asked me to put Abbie in the photo, I paused. Later that night, when we got home, Abbie said, "Michael, what was that pause?"

"That didn't mean anything," I said. "It was just a pause. I'm a pauser."

"Michael, if this isn't serious—"

"Of course it's serious. I love you."

"If you're not ready to get married, I don't know if I can do this."

"Abbie, I do want to marry you."

"When?"

Now, what I should have said was "Can we talk about this next summer?" What I did say was "Next . . . summer."

And that's how I got engaged, without actually getting engaged. I should have paid a little more attention to those episodes of *Wedding Story.* When you agree to get married "next summer," it is game on.

Abbie called everyone we knew and told them we were getting married. We started planning the wedding. I started having trouble breathing again, like when there was something in my bladder. I also began sleepwalking more frequently. I thought, *Maybe I should tell Abbie the truth,* and then I thought, *Maybe I'll eat dinner.* And I went with dinner.

A few months later I was asked to host the World Travel Awards at the Sandals Resort in St. Lucia. I had never heard of the World Travel Awards. I don't believe they are televised. Or even webcast. Or even really attended. Basically it's this completely made-up event where resorts reward themselves for being the best resort: "This year the award for best resort goes to . . . Sandals resort in St. Lucia!" Oh, that's funny. We're *at* Sandals Resort in St. Lucia. I hosted the event and the awards were presented by a cavalcade of minor celebrities, the most exciting of whom was Lydia Cornell, star of the eighties sitcom *Too Close for Comfort.*

But the reason I was most excited was that Abbie and I had never been on a vacation together and they were going to pay our way to this tropical resort. My whole life I had seen those commercials for the Caribbean where the water is unimaginably clear and as warm as bathwater and that voice says in a local accent, *"Caaahmmm to Jamaaaaaiiccaa!"* I'd watch these commercials and think, *I want to caaahm to Jamaica, but I can't afford it.*

Abbie and I had never been on a vacation partly because flying was the thing that terrified her the most. And partly because we had no money and the idea of a vacation is very strange when you have no money, because you're like, *My life usually costs a hundred dollars a week, but on vacation it's going to cost two or three thousand dollars a week.* So when I found out that I could take my girlfriend on one of these trips for free, I thought, *This is going to fix everything.*

Abbie had just started planning our wedding, but she could sense that I wasn't entirely invested in it. Thus I was going to smooth things over in St. Lucia.

We were picked up at the St. Lucia International Airport in a limousine. That seemed like a nice touch, until we started the driving part. St. Lucia is made up of beaches, high peaks, and rain forests. Which are all beautiful, but maybe not the best terrain for a Buick stretch limousine. We really could have used a Ford Explorer or Subaru Outback or even just a regular car with shocks. Abbie and I bounced up and down for the duration of a thirty-nine-mile drive from one end of the island to the other that ended up taking two and a half hours. In the course of this drive, Abbie and I started by picking apart the skills of the driver and then, eventually, each other. For two hours we criticized each other's jobs, families, even clothes. A lot of sentences started with "Well, if you're going to bring that up . . . ," and ended with something toxic. The phrase "Well, if you're going to bring that up" never ends with "I'm going to tell you I love you."

At the resort the bellman took our bags. Our room wasn't ready yet, so they sent us to the beach, where they gave us free drinks while we waited. We sat down at a table, inches from the soft, perfect sand, and Abbie said, "I think we should break up."

She only had to say it once. And I started tearing up like I had just witnessed the death of my best friend. And so did she. And we're sitting there on the beach, just crying. And we're looking out at the water. It was that perfect water. I could almost hear the *"Caaahmmm to Jamaaaaaiiccaa!"* coming off the ocean. The people at the tables next to us tried to pretend they couldn't hear us. We were that couple who was ruining other people's paradise vacation. Everything on the island was picture perfect except us. We could have had this argument at any coffee shop in New York, but we had to have it here. I sat there marveling at that water, crying. And so did Abbie. And that was day one of our Caribbean dream vacation.

Mitch Hedberg used to have a joke about how it's hard to get into an argument when you're staying in a tent: "What do you do? Slam the flap?" An island is even worse. It's not so conducive to breakups. You're on a strip of land in the middle of the ocean. What are you going to do, fly away? Maybe build one of those makeshift palm tree planes they made on *Gilligan's Island*?

For the first couple of days, we stayed in the hotel room. Abbie would disappear for hours at a time. When she got back, I'd ask where she'd gone and she wouldn't respond, as though I wasn't allowed to know. She had a point. We were literally too close for comfort. At a certain point I was upgraded to her business voice, which, since then, I've witnessed in a lot of breakups. All of a sudden she got cheery, distant, and professional.

"What can I do for you?

"Do you want to go for a walk tonight?"

And she's like, "We're not open past six."

"Okay. Do you want to get coffee?"

"If you'd like to admit you're wrong, press one. If you'd like to discuss your faults in detail, press two. If you'd like to spend less time on the road, press all the buttons at once and give up your dreams."

Finally I said, "Why don't we try to enjoy the things that we'd normally enjoy on an island? We're still friends, right?"

"Okay." We opened the hotel activity brochure and she suggested that we go scuba diving. This was insane. Abbie was almost as afraid of the water as she was of flying. And scuba diving is like flying underwater.

So we went scuba diving. Scuba diving transcends every rule you've ever held on to. Rules like "You can't breathe underwater" or "If you see a shark, you should run away." But we did it anyway. We swam through schools of thousands of colorful tropical fish. We even swam by sharks. And when we returned to the resort, I was euphoric and so was Abbie and I went to put my arm around her and she pulled away with her business demeanor and said, "That was fun."

That night we swam out to this floating trampoline. We were jumping up and down six or seven feet into the air and laughing. I thought, *This is just like it was before. This is going to work out.* Abbie made a giant leap into the water. And I jumped down after her and emerged right behind her putting my arms around her waist. And she pulled away. It was just inches away, but it felt like miles. And that was the distance I would feel for the rest of my time with Abbie.

The next day Abbie decided she wanted to leave the trip early. I had to stay, to host the World Travel Awards, but I said, "Okay." I asked the event coordinator if there was an easier way to get to the airport. He said there was a helicopter and I thought Abbie would say, "No way." But she said, "Great. A helicopter."

Later that day I walked Abbie to the helicopter landing and we both realized that the helicopter driver must have been fifteen years old. At most a young seventeen. The helicopter looked about as airworthy as the palm tree plane on *Gilligan's Island* and I thought Abbie would say, "No thanks," but she said, "Great. I'll see ya."

Abbie flew off in a rickety helicopter over the rain forest and hilly terrain of St. Lucia. She had left a relationship that by all estimation couldn't possibly end and left an island that seemed inescapable. She just flew away.

Abbie met someone named Nathan and they're still together today. And I met someone named Jenny and we're still together today. But the biggest difference was that Jenny was not okay with the jackal.

I got up on my bed and shouted, "There's a jackal in the room!" She said, "No, there isn't, and you have to see a doctor."

"I will, but right now I'm really busy."

That's how I justify not doing things that are important. I think, *I'm just so busy. People don't understand how busy I am. If people knew how busy I was, they'd know that I don't have time to see a doctor.*

One night Jenny and I fell asleep watching *Fight Club*. There's a scene in the movie where Brad Pitt holds down Edward Norton's hand and he's going to pour acid on it. And I had a dream that it was *my* hand. And I jumped out of bed and sprinted down the hall like I was in an action film, and I threw a chest of drawers in my wake because I knew that Brad Pitt is very cunning. I hit the elevator button and Jenny ran into the hall and shouted, "Michael, you're dreaming!"

"Brad Pitt was gonna pour . . . ," I insisted, but then I immediately apologized to Jenny and she said, "You have to see a doctor."

And I said, "I will." But I didn't.

I did however continue to read *The Promise of Sleep*. I skipped to a chapter on sleep disorders. There are seventy-eight known sleep disorders. Things that range from sleep apnea to night terrors to narcolepsy. Narcolepsy is terrifying because there are people who fall asleep at any time. There are female narcoleptics who fall asleep the moment they reach orgasm. I think you could call these women "men."

I came across something called REM behavior disorder, which is a condition where people have a dopamine deficiency. Dopamine is the chemical released into your body when you fall asleep that paralyzes you so you don't act on what's happening in your brain. I learned that people who have this deficiency have in rare instances been known to kill the person they're in bed with while remaining asleep. In other words, the person would have a dream that there was a burglar in the house and he would beat the burglar to death and then he'd wake and see that "the burglar" was in fact his wife and she's dead. And I read this and I thought, *That sounds a lot like what I have.*

And I still didn't see a doctor.

So it's January 20, 2005, and I'm in Walla Walla, Washington. I'm lying in bed at La Quinta Inn. I'm Googling myself, watching the news, and eating a pizza at the same time. And I fall asleep. And I have a dream that there is a guided missile headed toward my room and there are all these military personnel in the room and I jump out of bed and I say, "What's the plan?" And they say, "The missile coordinates are set specifically on you." And I decided in my dream and as it turns out in my life to jump out my window.

There are two important details here. One is that I was staying on the second floor. Two, the window was closed. So I jumped *through* the closed window. Like the Hulk. That's how I described it at the emergency room. I was like, "You know the Hulk? You know how he just kind of jumps through windows and walls?"

So I jumped *through* the window, and this is the hardest part to explain because people who have REM behavior disorder are physically able to do things they couldn't normally do because they don't feel any inhibition or pain. So I jumped through the window, fell two stories, landed on the front lawn of the hotel, got up, and kept running.

I'm running and I'm slowly realizing that I'm on the front lawn of La Quinta Inn in Walla Walla, Washington, in my underwear, bleeding. And I'm like, *Oh nooo.* But at that moment, the only thing I can think is that I'm relieved that I haven't been hit by the missile. *That would have been a disaster. At least I'm still in the game.*

It was the ultimate moment in my life where, in retrospect, I'm like, *WHAT THE HELL?* But at the time I was like, *I guess I'll walk to the front desk and explain what happened.* Fortunately the person working at the front desk was mildly retarded. And I say fortunately because he was completely unfazed by what had just happened. It's three in the morning. I'm standing at reception in my underwear, bleeding. The phones are ringing off the hook from people staying at the hotel who just saw the guy jump out the window. And I said, "Hello."

Because you have to start somewhere.

"I'm staying in the hotel. I had an incident and I jumped out my window and I need to go to a hospital." And I'll never forget his reaction. He just said, "All right." And I thought, *That's the best possible reaction I could receive at this juncture.*

So I drove myself to the hospital. I didn't see any other options. I was in the middle of nowhere. I wasn't going to knock on people's doors and be like, "Did you hear that guy screaming? That was me. I need a ride." So I drove myself, like that scene in *Reservoir Dogs.* I was bleeding and shouting and I had to explain what happened three times: to the receptionist, the nurse, and the doctor: "I'm the Hulk . . . I'm the Hulk . . . I'm the Hulk . . . " And one guy corrected me, "No, you're Bruce Banner." *Point taken, nerd.*

I was lying in a hospital bed with my clothes cut open and I could see glass shards coming out of my legs. It was the most pain I had ever felt. It was the physical pain of glass coming out of my legs combined with the emotional pain of *There's glass coming out of my legs . . . How did I get to a point where there's glass coming out of my legs?* It was cold. I was shivering. And I kept asking for warm blankets because I was afraid that if I moved, the glass would go deeper. I waited ten minutes and said to the nurse, "Is there a doctor? Because this is kind of an emergency. I know you guys have a lot going on, but I'd put my emergency head-to-head with anyone else's."

Eventually the doctor came and he took the pieces of glass out of my legs. Slowly. Very slowly. For about forty-five minutes. He pointed out glass right next to my femoral artery, and if the glass had cut it I would have bled to death. Then he said, "You should be dead."

And I said, "No, you should!"

I zinged him.

Because I'm a comedian.

He put thirty-three stitches in my legs and then I drove myself back to the hotel. And got a new room. Because I felt like that one had a stigma. And a slight draft. A few hours later I flew back to New York.

So that's the story. . . . But there's one more thing.

ONE MORE THING

I went to a doctor. And she sent me to what's called a "sleep study." This is basically a sleepover at the hospital. One of those sleepovers where they stick electrodes all over your naked body and a strange Russian man stares at you while you try to sleep.

The sleep study was on the sixth floor of a New York City building. This was a concern. I had just jumped through a second-story window the week before, and if it had been anything above four, I would have most likely died. It seemed ironic that I could feasibly sleepwalk out the window of the sleep center. Ironic, but not all that funny. My girlfriend Jenny told the Russian sleep technician, "We have to block the window with something."

"No problem," he said in his thick, unsettling accent. "We're watching him from the other room through these cameras."

"No, you don't understand," she said. "By the time you see him out of bed, he'll be out the window."

"This has never happened before," he said.

"We're pretty new to it ourselves," said Jenny.

I made it through the night, and after the doctor interpreted the results, I was diagnosed with REM behavior disorder, or RBD. It was recommended that I sleep in a sleeping bag and wear mittens—that way I couldn't open the sleeping bag. More important, I was prescribed Klonopin, an anti-anxiety drug that has surprisingly good results with people who suffer from RBD. At the doctor's suggestion, Jenny and I childproofed our bedroom. Whenever we traveled, Jenny insisted on placing large pieces of hotel furniture in front of the window. The cleaning people must have thought we were drug addicts or insane partiers because, in the morning, they'd walk into a Stonehenge of furniture.

It was a little lonelier when I was touring. I had to play a rigorous schedule of colleges and my agent Mike would have to call ahead and say, "Mike has to stay on the first floor." And inevitably they'd ask why, and he'd cover for me. He'd be like, "Because that's what Mike Birbiglia wants!" So I would show up and these people would hate me before we even met because I was this diva who had these strange requests that no one understood.

I never told these people the story. It's a hard story to tell in a few sentences. I tried with one student event coordinator.

"I jumped out a window in my sleep."

"You what?"

"I know. It's strange."

"Are you messing with me?"

"No."

"It seems like you're messing with me."

"No, uh . . . no. I have a sleep disorder and I didn't deal with it for a long time and it got worse and eventually it got so bad that I jumped out a window."

"Oh."

And then he looked at me sadly, and the conversation

couldn't return to a place of normalcy. I couldn't say, "No, but it's funny!"

The day I got home from the sleep study, Jenny told me that someone at her office had a sleep issue as well. This took me by surprise. I didn't think we were going to tell people about what had happened.

"You didn't tell people at your company about this, did you?" I asked.

"Well, yeah . . . I mean, I went straight to work from sleeping on the floor of the hospital. I was just telling my cubiclemates where I was."

"Don't tell people."

"Um . . . okay."

"People are going to think I'm insane. It's just not a good idea."

So Jenny didn't tell anyone. And I didn't tell anyone. And this thing happened where I started to feel this distance between me and everyone that I met. Just the slightest distance.

Around that time I book a show at a college in Boston. I arrive at the hotel the students have booked for me. It's on the seventeenth floor.

I'm seething with anger. But I don't want to tell them why. And I drive over to the school and stumble through my set. Backstage after the show one of the students who had booked me comes up to me and says, "Hey, that was great. We'd like to take you out for dinner."

And I say, "No."

He looks confused. And I say, "I have to drive two hours to my parents' house to sleep because you didn't book me on the first floor."

He looks even more confused and I shout at him.

"I HAD ONE FUCKING REQUEST. I HAD ONE THING THAT I ASKED FOR AND YOU FUCKED THAT UP!"

And I storm out and I'm driving home and it hits me that I just had my first "Goddammit, I'm eatin' pretzels" moment. And it destroys me.

I walk into my parents' house around 1:30 a.m. and my dad is up reading in the living room and I sit down on the couch. And I'm so upset that I tell him what just happened.

And he listens to me.

He says, "How have you been feeling since the sleepwalking incident?"

"Actually . . . not great." And I hesitate and then I say, "I'm starting to feel the slightest distance between me and everyone I meet."

My father thinks about this. And he says, "That's what happens when you get older."

And I *get* him.

I never thought this was going to happen. I'm twenty-nine years old and he's sixty-eight and he's sharing with me a truth that we've both experienced. It's something he knows and I know. And we both know. Right now, for that moment, we both know *stuff*.

So I tell him the whole sleepwalking story from the beginning. And that leads to other stories. I tell him things that I never thought I'd be able to tell my dad. A lot of stories I just told you. At the end of the conversation, my father stands up and he sits next to me on the couch. He puts his hand on my leg and says, "You know you're gonna have to take care of this.

You're gonna have to see a doctor regularly. And get a neurological workup. You need to take time off from the road. And learn to relax. You're going to have to deal with this because it's not going to deal with itself." And he walks into his bedroom. And when he's about to close the door, he looks back at me for a few moments.

And he says, "Whatever you do, don't tell anyone."

THANK-YOUS

First of all, don't read this unless you're scanning for your name. And if you are scanning, stop it. Please. Let me just say that I have gone unthanked on so many projects that I've contributed to. It doesn't make it right that I'm doing it to you. I'm just saying that accidents happen. Thank-you lists give me tremendous anxiety. *What if I leave someone out?* Then all of a sudden I'm Hilary Swank at the Oscars. That's not fair! I'm not Hilary Swank. I'm Tom Hanks thanking his gay teacher after *Philadelphia*. That was cool. Yeah, I'm Tom Hanks.

And now a list of my gay teachers:
Dave Becky and Stephanie Davis at 3 Arts, John Glavin, Rajeev Nath, Anaheed Alani, Michael Kavanagh, David Rosenthal, Peter Saraf, Mark Turtletaub, Maggie Kemper, Sean Conroy, Ivan and the late Miss Lucy, Lynn Shawcroft, Andrew Secunda, Catherine Burns, Barry Tyerman, Jamie Mendelbaum and Andy Galker, Marysue Rucci, AJ Jacobs, Michael Cogliantry. At S&S: Aileen Boyle and Tracey Guest. Thanks to all my friends at APA, UTA, The Moth, *The Bob and Tom Show*, and Comedy Central. Eli Gonda, Jeff Thom, and the *Sleepwalk with Me* crew; Joy Behar and *The View*; Mike Lavoie and James Fauvell; Ira Glass and the staff of *This American Life*; Nathan

Lane; Patti and Gina; and Mike Berkowitz, who convinced me to write this book.

A very special thanks to: Seth Barrish, Joe Birbiglia, Sarah Hochman—without you this book would not have been possible.

And Jenny the arctic fox. Without whom I would have no inspiration.

ABOUT THE AUTHOR

Mike Birbiglia is an actor, comedian, and storyteller. His critically acclaimed 2009 off-Broadway show, *Sleepwalk with Me,* was presented by Nathan Lane and was nominated for a Drama Desk Award and an Outer Critics Circle Award for Best Solo Performance. He has appeared in three solo Comedy Central Specials, including "What I Should Have Said Was Nothing." He has also recorded two albums with Comedy Central Records, *Two Drink Mike* and *My Secret Public Journal Live.* In addition to touring colleges and concert halls nationwide, Birbiglia appears regularly on *The Late Show with David Letterman.* He is a regular contributor on *This American Life, The Moth Radio Hour* and *The Bob & Tom Show.* Birbiglia lives in a fourth floor apartment with a broken elevator in New York City with his wife, Jenny. This is his first book.

THESE PEOPLE ALSO HOPE YOU ENJOYED READING *SLEEPWALK WITH ME*

"First, know that this book is well written and funny. Now, know that I hate cynicism. Hate it. This book is the opposite of cynicism. I love *Sleepwalk with Me*."

—Jeff Garlin, Prominent Comedic Person

"Funny. Very funny. Birbiglia is the child Woody Allen and Bob Newhart never had—please don't try to picture that 'encounter.' Smart and self-aware, with just enough perspective on his quirks and issues that you don't have to feel too sorry for him . . . as you laugh at and/or with him."

—Bob Odenkirk, creator and star of HBO's
Mr. Show with Bob and David

"Thank God for Mike Birbiglia and his sleep disorders. They have given us an immensely funny and poignant book about love, comedy, and pizza (among other things). Ignore him at your own risk."

—A. J. Jacobs, author of *My Life as an Experiment*

"Insightful, heartfelt, and comedic—what more could you want from a book? Mike Birbiglia is a unique and wonderful new voice in American theater and letters."

—Jonathan Ames, creator of HBO's *Bored to Death* and
author of *The Extra Man* and *Wake Up, Sir!*

"Mike Birbiglia is a good friend of mine but I'm still really happy when weird, bad things happen to him because I love hearing the stories."

—Seth Meyers, head writer and host of
Weekend Update, *Saturday Night Live*

"*Sleepwalk with Me* is a delightful stroll into the charming, intelligent, and accessible mind of Mike Birbiglia."

—Kristen Schaal, comedienne and costar of
Flight of the Conchords

"Mike Birbiglia might be the best comedian of our generation: smart, honest, and always painfully funny. He's the Rembrandt of awkwardness."

—Michael Ian Black, author of *My Custom Van*

"I was terrified by how much I related to Mike Birbiglia's stomach-churning, embarrassing stories of childhood, sex, and more. With writing that is fresh, starkly direct, and all his own, he exposes his real-life experiences—from the mundane to the extraordinary—in ways that made me laugh out loud at every page. So much fun to read . . . just be ready to cringe in self-recognition."

—David Wain, writer/director of *Role Models,
Wet Hot American Summer,* and *The State*

"*Sleepwalk with Me* is not your typical comedian-writes-book book. It's something else. It's laugh-out-loud funny from beginning to end, and it's a truly fascinating and bizarre story about a guy with a very real and a very unique problem. It completely blew me away."

—Michael Showalter, host of *Michael Showalter Showalter*
and author of *Mr. Funny Pants*

"Mike is my favorite kind of hero in his stories: always self-aware, usually awkward, sometimes sad, but never cynical or bitter. The truths he unpacks from his life ring like a bell."

—Adam Savage, co-host of Discovery's *MythBusters*

"*Sleepwalk with Me* is an amazing read—funny, insightful, heartbreaking, uplifting, terrifying at times, and very, very funny. Yeah, I said funny twice, but that's because it's really funny."

—Will Forte, writer and cast member,
Saturday Night Live

"Birbiglia's ability to translate this singular comic persona into seamless, Pringles-addictive prose is a radical achievement. You will want to play in Mike's childhood home, experience his delayed adolescence, and walk lucid through his dreams."

—Lena Dunham, writer and director of *Tiny Furniture*

"Mike Birbiglia's crafted a genuine rarity—a boisterous book you want to listen to, quietly."

—Patton Oswalt, author of *Zombie Spaceship Wasteland*

"Mike Birbiglia should be particularly commended on his sleepwalking story, which is most responsibly written, turning a non-funny situation into one of hilarity, and legitimizing such occasionally injurious behaviors as a normal part of human existence unrelated to psychiatric disorders."

—Mark Mahowald, M.D., coauthor of *Parasomnias*

"Mike Birbiglia's crafted a genuine rarity—a boisterous book you want to listen to, quietly."

—Patton Oswalt, author of *Zombie Spaceship Wasteland*

"Mike Birbiglia should be particularly commended on his sleepwalking story, which is most responsibly written, turning a non-funny situation into one of hilarity, and legitimizing such occasionally injurious behaviors as a normal part of human existence unrelated to psychiatric disorders."

—Mark Mahowald, M.D., coauthor of *Parasomnias*